# MICHAEL
## REFLECTIONS OF LIFE, LOVE, AND THE JOURNEY IN BETWEEN

Michael: Reflections of Life, Love, and The Journey In Between
Copyright © 2024 by Trea Jackson

Published in the United States of America

Library of Congress Control Number: 2024912477
ISBN   Paperback:      979-8-89091-713-3
ISBN   eBook:          979-8-89091-714-0

All rights reserved. No part of this publication may be reproduced, stored in a retrieval system or transmitted in any way by any means, electronic, mechanical, photocopy, recording or otherwise without the prior permission of the author except as provided by USA copyright law.

The opinions expressed by the author are not necessarily those of ReadersMagnet, LLC.

ReadersMagnet, LLC
10620 Treena Street, Suite 230 | San Diego, California, 92131 USA
1.619. 354. 2643 | www.readersmagnet.com

Book design copyright © 2024 by ReadersMagnet, LLC. All rights reserved.

Cover design by Tifanny Curaza
Interior design by Don De Guzman

# MICHAEL
### REFLECTIONS OF LIFE, LOVE, AND THE JOURNEY IN BETWEEN

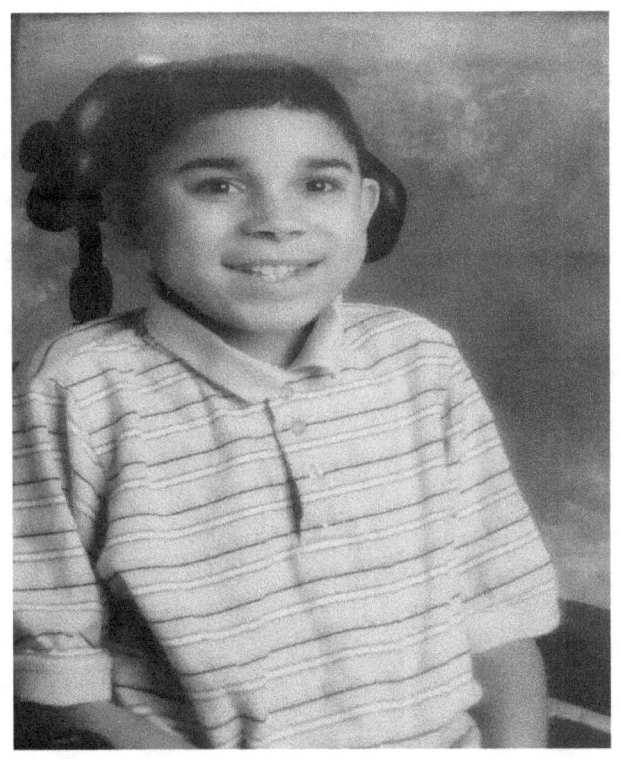

## TREA JACKSON

For my son, Michael, I love you very much. You are so missed. I will always cherish you in my heart forever.

For all the mothers that have lost children to Muscular Dystrophy, my heart understands your pain.

For my daughters that have lived without their brother and struggled to understand.

We cherish your love for life, your smile, and wisdom that you shared with all of us each and every day.

We miss you every day and, on your birthday, we celebrate your life.

# Preface

I was always going to share my stories about Michael while he was still here with us, but life was busy. But after he passed away, I was not so sure about a lot of things. Life seemed more complicated emotionally than ever. Michael had a lot to say, so I considered on and off about finishing the book that I started for my son. There were many stories entangled in my life, Michael's and our ever-changing life that impacted us.

So, I tell the story as it is meant to be told. It can only be told from a mother's point of view, experiences both past and present, and this is our story. I start from the beginning, and life as it was happening. There are moments of immense joy, sadness, and struggle. There are thoughts and emotions of happiness, sadness, frustration, and great despair. We made the best of our circumstances and created memories of joy. I had to create a quality life for Michael and the other children without the disease. I had to put in the back of my head what was going to happen to my Michael. The gateway to my deepest sorrows had to stay hidden away or written in my journal.

Having grown up in foster care and while in care, I was abused and neglected. This made me stronger to deal with my son being diagnosed with Duchenne's Muscular Dystrophy. I had to live with day-to-day life everchanging with the uncertainties and feelings of sadness, frustration, and disappointment. I was still living in care when Michael was born. So, there was no support from the Department of Children and Family Services, (DCFS) or anyone else for that matter. I had very few connections, but no one was living close to give that emotional support. I felt alone. But, because of growing up this way in care (foster care) I did not encounter the shock of total disappointment. I treated it as another challenge that

I had to work through with the two children at my side. It was an experience that I learned from, but I would never wish this kind of pain on anyone. Michael always said, "When you remember me, think of…well you can read the poem."

Ashley and Michael

## MICHAEL: REFLECTIONS OF LIFE, LOVE, AND THE JOURNEY IN BETWEEN

Michael said, when You Remember Me…

When you remember me, remember me as the ocean waves so free,

Remember me as the leaves on the tree that blow so freely,

Remember my smile that lit up people's lives,

Remember me as the tiger who hunts to survive,

Remember my love for life, my desire to keep going, and my wit that drew everyone in,

Remember my sense of humor that made the world laugh, sometimes with me, and sometimes at me,

Remember the lessons I gave so freely so that others could appreciate,

Remember me as the happy little boy who could run so freely,

Remember me as the brother who loved so freely,

Remember me as the son who never frowned,

Remember me as the plane that flies in the sky,

Remember me as the child who wanders in the way in search of adventure,

Remember me as the curly haired boy who never was beaten down,

Remember my smile, and the goodness in my heart,

Remember to let my spirit and legacy live on,

Remember me as the ocean blue sea that brings comfort to me,

Forget me not, for I am the one who is finally free,

Just like the fish in the sea,

Do not be sad when I am gone, just look in the sky and I will always be right beside you.

## CHAPTER ONE

# THE BEGINNING

Michael came into the world on a rainy summer day. When Michael was first born, he looked like a teddy bear already to hug. To me, he was perfect! Yes, I know all parents say and think that, but he really was. I don't what it is about Michaels? They just have this extra light, and they shine more than anything else. He would need all the light he could get to create the energy needed for his journey, which became our journey. He was so adorable--he had brown skin, brown curly hair, and big brown eyes. Michael definitely had my white genes mixed with Hispanic and Native American. He had that Hispanic look, but I was exceptionally light skinned. Michael got his color from his father who was Liberian and had very dark skin. Rarely do people see much of my non-white genes. Michael had a little bit of brown color to him, but I was told that more would come later, so his nurse who was Nigerian told me.

The emotional stress caught up with me shortly before I went into labor. I had no one here for me, so there was no support. I never imagined that things would go this way, but sadly they did. How I ended up alone, I will explain later. It was a long difficult delivery that lasted for two days. I thought he was never going to come out. I needed some help when he started to go into distress. He was quickly delivered using forceps. For that reason, he was born with a scar on his right cheek from the forceps, and a broken right shoulder. He was quickly taken to ICU. Later that day, he was brought back to me. When he looked up at me, he looked so cute with those cheeks. He was a little teddy bear. A few hours later, he was taken from me again, after I tried feeding him, but his temperature was too low.

He was having trouble maintaining what they called a normal body temperature for a newborn. Next thing I know is a nurse rushing into the room for me to sign some form--giving permission to a medical procedure. Michael needed a spinal tap to rule out Meningitis. This was a nightmare for me. Afterwards, he was put on antibiotics for two weeks.

I was too young and felt that I was a failure as a person. Didn't really get that I was now responsible for this little life. It was surreal that this baby was here, so I didn't feel like a mother. There was no motherly connection to this baby. I hope this feeling will get better, but if it does not, I might consider adoption again because I had nothing to offer this baby. I had no money and no place to even take this baby home. Suddenly, all those negative words from former foster parents came rushing back in my head. I felt hopeless, worthless, and without a doubt-a failure. I was just a foster child waiting for a spot in the Independent Living Program, but I was utterly lost.

I was not ready to be a mother, but here I was-ready or not. Foster children—both former and current are the recruiting grounds for creating second generation foster children. Some are allowed to stay with their mothers but are locked up in the same system making it the breeding ground for single mother births and questionable parenting skills. It's not that children immersed in the foster care system can't be good parents, but they may need extra coaching or parenting classes. You have to remember based on the foster care experience; the new mother may have had no positive role models. From whom do we learn? But in general, even outside the foster care system while I was growing up, parents just checked out for whatever reason it may be. Children were left to teach and fend for themselves. This is the result of no-parenting.

During the pregnancy, I had put the baby with an adoption agency. They found three sets of parents which included one single father interested in adopting my baby. I didn't know it at first, but the single father was a high-profile celebrity. I didn't want my child to grow up in a bubble and have grand expectations while being labeled because of who his father was. He wanted to meet with me and even invited me to his house which was located on a huge 2000-acre estate. I picked the single father because of how much he loved children. Two of the other married couples were also high-profile and wealthy, but they also had 2-3 nannies. Sadly, they were barely around to raise the other kids. It looks like they wanted a trophy baby. So, I didn't think they would be good. My decision to give this baby to the single father felt good. He really wanted the baby and was an excellent father. I was quite impressed with him, he did however, have one nanny which he only used when he absolutely had to. He really enjoyed the entire parenting thing. I had a strong connection to this person too, as this became a surprised reconnection.

Everything was going well, but then it was decided that he would not be permitted to adopt the baby. The agency found some old accusations and questioned whether the father was gay. The other two sets of possible parents backed out when they learned the baby was from a Black man. So, in the end I had no adoptive parent or parents for the baby. He would sit in foster care until a family was found. I didn't want to put him through what I went through, so I decided to keep him, at least for the time being. I was hoping that I would meet a childless couple who would decide to adopt him and give him a better life. I did remain in contact with the single father who was going to adopt the baby. He was always offering money to help, but I refused. He remained a great friend and rock of support.

I already failed when I came home, and Michael stayed at the hospital. If you would have asked me then, did I think something was wrong with him? I would have said, "No." He acted and looked very normal, nevertheless, I had no idea what was lurking in Michael's little body. It would be a few years before the most devastating news would be revealed. From the moment he arrived home, all he did was cry. I used to beg him to just stop crying, even if it was just for a little while. It turns out that Michael had colic and it would eventually get better. The unfortunate part was that it would take some time. I had to learn patience, I guess.

Things were rough, I was basically homeless when he arrived. My co-worker, Sam, who I thought was my friend, allowed me to stay with her. This arrangement was an exchange for watching her two children, Emily, and Ethan, who were ages 5 and 7. I was given a room in the house across the hall from Emily. Due to my plans of adoption, I didn't have much to nothing for the baby. I had no idea what I was even going to do. The WIC program gave me formula, some clothes, blankets, diaper bag, diapers, and a bassinet. I went to the dollar store for some essentials that Sam said the baby would need. Everything about Michael was normal. He was a happy baby turned toddler. Michael was always making everyone laugh with his presence. He loved to take walks and play at the park. Michael shined like the brightest star. I don't know what it is about "Michaels," but like I said before, they all seem to shine and light up the world one way or another.

My friend had some issues going on with her soon to-be ex-husband. He found out that his wife had a boyfriend who would spend the night at the house while the kids were in the other room. One day, while they were on the way to church, the father snatched the kids from their mother. Of course, she was really upset about the situation, but continued seeing the guy. So as a result, her aunt who owned her building, told her that she had to move. By then, I got a job and was in college part-time. I was able to move to an apartment and share the rent with her. But things didn't go well. She was spending all her time with her boyfriend and wanted me to pay more rent, so I moved out.

I found a one-bedroom far away from her. She threatened to get me cut off from programs that were helping me, just to be mean. She was angry because her kids were with their father, but how was that my fault? I was already paying for all the food in the house and paying half the rent/utilities. The sad thing was that I really had nobody, but I wasn't going to get into the drama. She even had a girl about the same age as me living in her room, paying nothing.

I was just waiting for the call from my caseworker that I got into the Independent Living program. I needed it more than ever, now that the baby was here, and the short-lived marriage to Alex, was annulled. My attempt to escape from the foster care system failed and this older man went after me because I was a young girl, naïve, and had never been with anyone. I was targeted when he lured me in and he used me, but he had no intention of being a father. He was already with someone and had another life. I was devastated and heartbroken. Why would he do this to me? I thought it was love, but it was not. He married me to make it look right and I was just going to be the second wife, I guess. He started to hit me. I found myself stuck in the moment of dysfunction once again in my life and because of my past—I felt I deserved it. There was some other drama going on as well, but in the end, it was all worked out to where we all parted ways.

DCFS filed child support on my behalf for Michael. I had not seen Alex since he came to the hospital when Michael was born; this was when he was trying to convince me that I should give the baby up for adoption. He claimed he was a different person and he got counseling for his issues with hitting people. I refused to give in because just wanted to get rid of the evidence that he got me pregnant. There was a baby which he wanted to hide from the other wife. He told everyone I was much older than I really was to avoid telling the truth that I was underage. Everything was wrong with the so-called relationship, the lies, the marriage, and the fact he was trying to cover it up. He came to talk to me before court. I actually jumped back when he approached me because I was scared. He asked me to just drop the child support thing and he would pay child support off the record and give me an apartment free of charge that his mother owned.

I had no choice with child support because DCFS was involved, and they were my guardians. But he managed to work out a deal with the judge stating he would send the payments to them every week as long as they don't take it from his check. He gave some boo-hoo story about how his ex-wife now, will keep his older son from him if she finds about the child support. Alex had to deny the baby because she was going to come after me out of jealousy. Wow, he is quite convincing, and the judge bought it. Who knows if any of that was even true. Alex gave me an apartment and I didn't have to pay anything. Was he for real or just lying again? I told DCFS I had somewhere to stay until I could get into the program that was taking forever. I felt safe until my baby's father did what he did and things after that would never be the same. There are some things that are unforgivable.

I know many won't understand why I would have another baby.

Many never knew the truth that led to this occurrence. I kept my feelings deep down inside. The next March, Michael was joined by a sister, Ashley. She was supposed to come in May, but she came early. Ashley looked more Asian and darker, more so than Michael did at birth. When I brought her home, Michael's eyes got big. He was an excellent big brother. Michael loved to help feed her but had a little bit of difficulty because she kept moving around and he was so little. He loved his sister and loved having someone to play with. From the time they woke up in the morning they were together. They rarely fought about anything, except for Michael's cars. His cars were his favorite and they kept disappearing. He was looking everywhere for them but could not find them. Michael loved to watch Bob the Builder and all the other PBS shows. This was the only thing that they did not do together. Michael was so happy and was just a pleasant child, overall.

I felt I was too young to be a good mother. I didn't have the skills that were needed. Then there was the loneliness, despite having Michael and the baby. I was a full-time college student and worked full-time at Sears. Now, I was living in a domestic violence shelter . In August, I moved to a new apartment with Michael and Ashley. In court, the marriage was found not to be valid because I was underage. He lied about everything on the marriage license. Alex wanted forgiveness, but what he had done couldn't be overlooked.

It all went downhill fast, and just as fast as it started. But it was based on lies. He knew I had nobody, and I was searching for that love. I thought life would be perfect together but found out he was not who he pretended to be. I was young and so naïve. I found out I was pregnant two months after we got married. I was only with him once, and then he claimed he worked two jobs, so I didn't see him for two months. Why would a new husband want to be away from his wife for two months? I knew something was up when he did not want me to keep the baby, so I was confused. He started fighting with me, saying I was a mistake. After that, he attacked me verbally and then physically. His violent outbursts came so frequently. He only came to my apartment to beat on me in hopes that I would lose the baby. I had bruises all over me. He had no idea that I wasn't even keeping the baby.

My thinking was that the baby would go to good parents. But he didn't care.

One night, I feared for my life and the life of our unborn baby, so I ran away. First to a shelter and later to a friend's house. I found out what all the drama was about a few months before Michael was born. He had another lady in his life who was the mother of his other child. They broke up right before he met me, but they got back together a few weeks after we got married. That is why he didn't want me to have the baby. So, after I was too far along, he begged me to give the baby up for adoption, or that we could get a lot of money for the baby. I didn't want him to get into this adoption process because then he might just change his mind. It went in that direction when he suggested that I sell the baby. Yes, he was crazy. He wanted me to sell the baby. I was a foster child, so I had nothing. For a moment, I thought I would have something after the baby was here, but then reality set in, and I knew I was doing the right thing; I needed to get away from him. He was a loose cannon.

He would always tell me that he was not done with me. It is so hard to tell the truth when domestic issues arise. I really felt it was my fault, because falling into the systematic patterns of abuse is extremely easy for me due to being a survivor of child abuse. So, I felt just as trapped as when I was a child. I never wanted any harm to come to Michael. But would this man really hurt his son? So, when I least expected it, he was standing in my living room. He reeked of alcohol. What happened to me is what happens to a lot of young girls who just cannot get away from an abusive partner. I was violated physically, emotionally, and what lead to another pregnancy. I called the police, which proved to be pointless, and did not want to talk about the details of what happened. I had a newborn son in the crib. He did this violent act right in front of him. The police made it okay what he did because we were once a couple. They claimed nothing happened here. I requested a female officer, but because it was the near the end of their shift, I was refused. I was given the advice to change the locks and to move. I was left there with no medical treatment, all bruised up, while feeling all broken and damaged. I just refer to what happened as "the incident."

The next day, I went into Planned Parenthood to get some help. They were extremely helpful by giving me the attention I needed to recover. I was at a domestic shelter for a while with Michael. After that, I got my own apartment through the Independent Living Program, got a job, and enrolled back in college. I had to push through all this trauma. I was often scared, but especially when I found out I was pregnant. I did not want to tell anyone what happened, so I just told people in my exceedingly small inner circle that I found out I was pregnant after ending our marriage. He was living a double life once again, but not with me. I just wanted him to leave me alone and if that meant no child support, then I would accept that. It's better to struggle alone than end up dead.

A few months before I was to give birth to a daughter, he came to confront me at a store. As he came close, I moved away from him. He tried to calm me with his manipulative words. He even tried to convince me, while his son was in the cart, that things got out of hand last time he saw me. Alex really wanted things to work out, but he had been drinking. He would not admit what he did, but made the request that we can be a family? He must be crazy. I shut it down, "I don't think so." This was over and the paperwork was sealed. Why was he here? What did the other wife kick him out?

The truth is, we were already a family with or without him. He was a cheater amongst the other things he had done to me. This was not the first time he had violated a young girl, I later found out. He did not like the answers I was giving him, so he raised his hand at me and then grabbed me. When he looked up and saw he had an audience, he started to hesitate. So, very aggressively, he said, "This is not over!" He just walked out of the store. I was relieved to see him walk away.

How did this happen to me? You often reflect on what events have already happened in your life. I guess for me, I really was desperate for love after never receiving it in my childhood. I really wanted to grow up to be beautiful, so I would get a husband who would love and adore me? I always wanted to be with only one guy my entire life. I was saddened by how things turned out. So, I just pushed it off on the fact things happen for a reason. I vowed off all guys, so I would never be hurt again.

I went into labor early with Ashley and delivered her prematurely. A friend, (let's call him Mason), showed up to the hospital. He was present while I brought my daughter into the world. He was such a great friend and was so supportive. He could not stand Alex whatsoever. I had to pick a name for my daughter, which I had not done yet. So, we were watching *The Fresh Prince of Bel-Air,* and then it came to me. I decided to name her Ashley. It was a close toss-up between Hillary and Ashley. But, can you imagine, "Daddy, credit card please." So, when I brought Ashley home—it was a new apartment far away from crazy Alex. So, I hoped Michael would not remember any of this harmful stuff that happened to me. I hope I finally broke free of this man that I thought I loved so much. I felt so betrayed and let down, but I had to keep moving forward.

# CHAPTER TWO

# FINDING MY STRENGTH

Being a single mother was demanding work. I had to get up at 6am while Michael and Ashley were still sleeping. I would go to school and then work after that. I had to take two buses to school and another bus to work. A neighbor, named Joan, would come and care for my little ones. She loved my kids like they were her own grandchildren. I worked until 9pm most days, except for on Friday and Saturday-- I worked until 3pm. Sunday I was off, so I tried to spend time with the babies. I had to do shopping and laundry that day too, so they came along. But living on the third floor was quite a journey with the kiddos, laundry, and groceries, but after a few trips I was in for the day. I would do homework and study until one in the morning, sometimes two.

    I had to get some help from the Department of Human Services with childcare and medical. The office I went to was awful. They have to be the worst office in the state. The dehumanizing system treated people like trash. Their father kept quitting his job, so he would not have to pay child support. I really did not like to ask for help from anyone. I had a lot of disappointments growing up, so I learned just to rely on myself. I felt I had messed things up in my life and for the children. Ashley was only a baby and would never know her father or the terrible things he did. I never wanted her to know the terrible truth of what he did to me that created her. Michael was only a toddler but didn't notice anything out of place with all this stuff going on. I was struggling at times to be a parent, but tried my hardest to love, care for and protect them. I knew that going to college was my only way out of all this and to make a better future. At age 2, Michael started walking a little funny--like a waddle walk. He started to walk slower than usual. Then he started having trouble getting up the stairs. We lived on the third floor, so he had to walk up three flights, but he struggled a whole lot. Michael looked like a little old man going up the stairs and he was only two years old. I took him to the doctor, and they told me that nothing was wrong with him. They said that all little boys go through this lazy stage. I believed what the doctor said and just went along with it. But something was not right. Mothers just know, right? It was right after that when Michael had an even slower waddle walk. It was kind of cute, but when I looked at the other kids his age, they didn't seem to have that walk. I sensed there was more going on. But what?

I started a new job in November at Toys R US. I was hired as temporary help for the Christmas season and also worked at Sears full-time. They said I was so impressed that they wanted me to stay on to be the Juvenile Department World Leader. This job was offered to me full time and paid more than Sears, so I took it. I really enjoyed my job helping parents with the gift registry and answering questions about baby products.

I also met a guy at Toys R US and his name is Manny. He was a good friend. Manny lived on the Southside of Chicago and had been working at the store since he was sixteen. He seemed like a nice guy. It was hard being a single mother with two young children. The neighbor had started complaining from downstairs, that the kids were jumping. She even called the police one early morning. Four officers came, like it took four officers to oversee this. Their time could have been used on more important things. She went on and on telling the officers that it was so loud she couldn't sleep. The officers didn't seem to understand what to do. They didn't know the real reason for what was going on. The babysitter of my kids often complained about the noise from downstairs during lunch time. So, I let the officers know that the kids go to bed early because they cannot take naps due to her teenage daughter having her lunch friends over. There are about sixteen of them who come over, play loud music, drink and I even smell the herbal pot smell coming from their unit.

She was quick to deny it. The police seemed more interested in what was going on downstairs. She became more furious. One of the officers said that we need to get along. Before leaving, they told me to call the police when those kids get there in the afternoon. I just nodded in agreement, not knowing if I would truly call them. I couldn't believe that she called the police on the kids.

I was remarkably busy and didn't have time to deal with her drama. I was so busy being a mother, full-time student, and worker. She needs to be more concerned with what her daughter is doing and stay out of my business. My kids were so little, and they did get energetic at times throughout the day. I teach them to have respect, but they will get it one day. I hope soon I can move, perhaps to something on the first floor. Then the kids can have some freedom. Ashley had so much energy, but now Michael was struggling to keep up. I was so concerned that something was wrong.

In March, Ashley turned one and was already walking. Now she followed Michael all over the house. He would try to jump up quickly, grab himself, and waddle to the bathroom. When he came out, he would say, "That was a close one." Of course, as a parent I would suggest to him to go to the bathroom earlier. But he did that every time he had to go. Ashley was like a ball of energy. Michael wasn't and he looked so tired. Just walking from one side of the house to the other wore him out. He was now falling down a lot too. He would just fall with no rhyme or reason. I couldn't figure it out. I took him to the doctor and then that doctor sent him to another one. I kept getting the same answer, "There is nothing wrong. Everything is fine."

Everything is not fine, and it was just around the corner to find out the truth. Truth is never really what you really want, no matter what anyone says. The truth hurts, but it does have the habit of releasing us and setting us free. We all want to know the truth, but when we get told-- it sends us into orbit. It sometimes sends us into action and gives us direction. It's never usually what we want to hear. It's like you want both, you want the truth, but you want to be subjective about the truth. It doesn't work that way, unfortunately.

As the year went on, Michael kept falling, was tired, and could barely walk upstairs. Ashley would try to help him, but she was so small that it didn't work out so well. Eventually, things got so rough that I was totally stressed out. I was even tempted to stop going to college full time and take another job. Daycare costs were expensive. I had to pay $100 weekly, pay for food and other necessities for the children, utilities, and bus cards. The rent was being covered by DCFS and I still received $400 a month from the Independent Living Program, but I was going to age out soon and wouldn't receive that money. I was unkindly warned that when that money and help disappears-I would be homeless, and my children would be taken away to the foster care system. So instead of preparing us—they leave us with extraordinarily little preparation for a very uncertain future. Many former foster children become homeless and in jail within one year of aging out.

There were some programs I just didn't qualify for because I was under the title of DCFS. I did however qualify for the WIC program and there was a food pantry down the street ran by Buddhist Monks. They were so nice to me and my children. There was one of them, his name was Tyen. He would always help me home with the food and speak to me on the way. One day, he asked me about the children's father. I just told him that he was gone. He had great sympathy, and he was happy to hear I was in school. He spoke a lot about Buddha and his teachings about wisdom. Due to our talks, it gave me hope and I did not quit school.

So, I applied for food stamps to help with the food costs for the children. I waited the entire day at the Illinois Department of Human Services (DHS) office and was interviewed by the meanest-most anti-social caseworker you could ever meet. She was just rude. You felt like a number in a system that really did not care one way or another. I sat and witnessed many rude caseworkers that treated everyone just as bad. This Skokie office had a bad rap for negative behaviors towards the public they serve. I cannot believe the state actually hires people who act like this. Over the time I was serviced by the office, I did meet one woman who was nice. We will call her Ms. R, which of course, is not her real name.

After many trips of spending my entire day at the office, I was told that I couldn't get anything until after I age-out. I did get info on the childcare assistance program, which was immensely helpful. Now I can get some help with those costs. I was forced to go to child support child support again soon after. Several months later, I received a check for $6000. The money came from the IRS interception of his taxes. I was so excited that finally I got something for the children. Then I started receiving regular payments every two weeks in the amount of $240. This helped me a lot, but it was a struggle to get to this point. You must learn to maneuver through the system and that is the hardest part. Once you learn how to do that-- you get to the things that can help. There are roadblocks that sometimes you feel are intentionally put there to try to discourage you from even trying. I would have to say that Child Support Enforcement and DHS--I saw these same roadblocks. I swear if I ever work for either of these agencies, I will never treat people badly just to crush their spirits and to get rid of them.

## CHAPTER THREE

# FEELING ALL BROKEN

A month before I was to age-out I lost my job. So, I became homeless a few months later. I went to a shelter with the children which was exceedingly difficult. I was offered an opportunity to be part of a program for children who aged out of the foster care system and end up homeless like myself. They helped me with counseling, getting employment, and with getting enrolled back into college. I had to take a semester off due to becoming homeless. I found a new place to live with the children and the program even paid the first 3 months of rent.

I found that I had a lot of unresolved issues from being abused and the foster care system. I was scarred by the system that was supposed to protect me. I was not alone. Talking about all this was very emotional and extremely overwhelming. I started to write journals of what I went through and decided I would finish the series of books that I had started about my abuse and struggles in the foster care system.

I met a female friend at work. She was a struggling single mother with a baby, named, Jonas, the same age as Ashley. Her name was Nessa. She was from Florida and was staying with her boyfriend, named Junior. She had an older daughter, named Kate, who lived with her grandparents in Florida. She had her first child at fourteen. She wanted to leave her boyfriend, so she moved in with me. We split the rent, utilities, and food bill. Her boyfriend came over quite a bit to pick his son up and that sort of thing. Nessa and Junior would fight a lot and slip out a lot of curse words, which I was not used to. He thought that Nessa and I were dating, so he felt rejected. He eventually gave up, but he was a good father to Jonas.

Things stayed the same. It was like a repetitive pattern. I was exhausted from all the work and college. I was taking classes at Wright College but had no idea what I wanted to do. I was thinking Psychology and to be a therapist or something like that. I knew that before I could help other people, I had to heal myself. I felt at times, I was just stuck in the moment in which the trauma started. I refer to that as the moment when I became self-aware of what was happening to me. This sent me into a shutdown mode where I built a wall around me to protect myself. This was a rough time for me.

I just wanted a way out of all this stress and pressure. I wanted to make sure that the kids were being taken care of. I wanted a career not just a dead-end job. The kids were with the babysitter all day and they did not like that. They wanted me. It was awfully hard doing all this stuff with limited help. Going to work, and then going to school. Then, on top of that, there was all the homework, which had no end. I wanted to give up at times, but just when I felt this was it, I found some strength to go on. And so, I did.

All the doctor's visits added to the stress. Michael continued having issues with the everyday things that people just take for granted. He was falling and could not get up. He was having trouble walking around the house now. There was something wrong and I just knew it. I tried to push it out of my head just to get through the day. I wanted not to think about it, but somehow it was always there. I had a full plate with life, and I was terrified. Out of desperation, I started calling doctor after doctor trying to get answers. I kept getting the same answers which were no help at all. After taking Michael to the doctor one day, I ran into Alex. He was a medical car driver for the hospital where Michael went for testing. I asked him what he thought could be wrong and if anything, genetically ran in the family. I do not know why I even bothered. In a moment where he could have attempted to be a good guy, he just didn't. But he did say that if something was wrong with him, he did not get from his side of the family. That was his answer. Michael would have to be taken care of no matter what. It was just a question.

Nessa left for Florida with Jonas, six months after she moved with me. She had family over there that could help her. She also missed her daughter Kate. I did miss her a lot when she left. We would sit up and have girl talk after the kids went to bed. I would be working on homework while she would talk about her family. Junior was not happy that his son was going back to Florida and even asked Nessa to leave him here with him. But she refused and left on the plane.

Alex found me and would show up to the apartment every so often uninvited. He was generally high from the drugs and alcohol. Restraining orders did nothing for me. Sometimes, he was so high that he tried to get me to go to the bedroom. That was not going to happen. But other times, he would get violent and would smack me. I would try to put the kids in a room before it escalated, but often they were left to witness his rage. He would leave right after any violent outbursts. With Nessa there he would not come around much. The last incident led to him not paying anymore child support.

In Spring 2001, child support stopped, so I went back to court. Alex attempted to charm the judge by saying that the kids were not his and to dismiss the case on those grounds. I explained to the public defender assigned to the case that I just needed the child support, but not if he is allowed harass me for these kinds of unwanted requests. I was so scared of this man and what he would perhaps do again if he had the chance. The courts did not know what he had already done, and I did not want to tell them. They did not need to know how Ashley was conceived, and I never wanted her to know until perhaps she was old enough to understand-- like after 18 or perhaps never. She is my daughter and I love her. But Alex was up to something to try to deceive the courts to get out of paying child support.

So, as the case proceeded, the judge was not buying it. So, I had Ashley with me, but he never even looked her way. Maybe he was feeling too guilty for what he had done. I was holding Ashley while we were in court. She took a long look at Ashley and then back at Alex. She said, "The proof is in the pudding." She meant she looked just like him, which she was correct. He got smart on her obviously and he thought it would work. He requested a DNA test. The judge was smarter, she agreed to the DNA test, but if the test came back positive; he would have to pay for the cost of the test.

Then she looked down and was reading something off a paper. There was a section of the birth certificate for Ashley where the father's name was absent and where the section was filled out concerning the conception of the baby which raised the judges' eyebrows. So, she allowed the DNA test for Ashley only. The test came back positive that he was indeed the father. He was arrested a few days later for what he had done to me. He received 10 years, but only served 6 months. He got out on good behavior. What does good behavior have to do with the evil he did to me? He came straight for me after being released but ran off when he heard the police sirens.

In Summer 2001, Nessa showed up back to Chicago with Jonas. Everything was going well. She enrolled at Wright College with me. She worked at McDonald's in the evening time while I worked at Toys R Us. Nessa found out that she was pregnant before she arrived in Chicago. The father of the child wanted nothing to do with her, Junior was furious that she was pregnant with his ex-best friend's baby. Junior seemed to know the guy well. She was so happy that she was having his baby. Nessa stayed another few months before leaving to go back to Florida again.

Michael started early head-start at the at Chappell Grade School-- just a few blocks from the house. I put Ashley at the daycare located at the YMCA down the street. There were issues with Michael, so the teacher said. She talked to me when I picked him up. She was complaining about everything he did that day. You would think that she dealt with all kinds of issues that kids had? Children are all different. She thought that Michael was not ready for school. She said he was having trouble walking, going up the stairs, he had no interest in the learning process, and wanted to play all day.

I was quite concerned with the teacher making such statements after knowing him for one day. Over the next week, I got a call from the principal, the social worker, the psychologist, and the special education team. They were going to evaluate him and see if this was the best school for him. I just went along with it and really did not know if I had a choice. There was something wrong with Michael.

I did agree with that. But what was shocking, was what seemed like concern at First, quickly turned into mean words from the school staff. Michael got hurt one day and I was called. A kid pulled his chair out from behind him when he was sitting down. The librarian even had comments for me when I picked him up, calling him a troublemaker and attention seeking. That is great when people who barely know your child make such harsh analyzing comments. They have no idea about what they are talking about. They did not want him at the school.

Over the next few months, they put him through all sorts of tests to attempt to find out what was going on. Then outside school there was the endless doctor's appointments with tests that just kept coming. The blood work, CT, MRI, EKG, EEG, and cardiologist. He has been to seven physical therapists, two neurologists, six pediatricians, and still nothing. First it was Autism, developmental disability, and Cerebral Palsy. But, as soon as he was diagnosed, then another doctor would rule it out.

Then we were back to trying to figure out what was wrong with Michael. The school kept singing the same tune of how they wanted to help him. I started to have my doubts, especially when the principal called and said that Michael could not go on a field trip because it involved walking. There was no accommodation for Michael, he was just left out. On the other hand, he could not walk too far now. He would just fall down after just a few steps every time he walked. He now walked on his tippy toes, and when he got up from the floor he struggled. It was as if he were balancing his hips slowly before he would rise completely. But he still deserved to go on field trips and have fun as a child. Was he to be denied being treated the same as the other children? It looks like for now that would be the case. There is a meeting scheduled to determine what placement would be good for Michael. They call this meeting the IEP (Individual Educational Plan).

In December, I sat at table full school officials, including Michael's teacher, principal, social worker, psychologist, developmental specialist, and the special education teacher. They all went around taking their turns telling me what they thought of my son. They were all analyzing Michael so much that they forgot about him being a real-life boy with some serious unknown issues. They went on and on, and then gave their recommendations, as they called it. They even became doctors, telling me what they thought was wrong with him. They would say that it was Autism, Cerebral Palsy, or Multiple Sclerosis, and then put their foot in their mouths as each one was ruled out by the real doctors repeatedly.

But truthfully, the doctors either wanted to be treated like god's or didn't want to be bothered. They never could admit that they didn't know. After all this talk, they decided that Michael was delayed and needed to go to a special school that could help him. He needed to be in a smaller classroom, and he needed special education. However, his issue was physical. I warned them to wait before they set this decision into motion. We had a doctor's appointment at Children's Memorial next month. He was to see two new doctors, Dr. M and Dr. S, to find a possible diagnosis. The school didn't want to wait and wanted Michael to be transferred as soon as possible.

That meant Monday morning Michael would be transferred to LA Moyne Grade school. He would be bused to the school every day. It was clear they wanted to get rid of him. They saw him as a problem and wanted to remove him as soon as possible. So, this was not a recommendation, it was an order. I was given his paperwork and told to go to the school to enroll him.

## CHAPTER FOUR

# HE HAS WHAT?
# NOTHING WILL EVER BE THE SAME

His new school was a self-contained room and ten other kids were worse off than Michael. They didn't talk at all and had serious problems. Michael was different though and he wanted to learn. But this thing, whatever it was, was holding him back. They weren't going to teach him anything. He was stuck in this little room with no way out, and it was the school system that got to decide what was good for him. I was not allowed in that decision making with the school. The school became the judges of a child they barely knew and for Michael, I knew they were wrong. There was nothing wrong with his mind, but they wouldn't listen.

The first week he was at the school, I got a call from the Physical Therapist. She told me that something wasn't right with Michael. Of course, I knew that. She said she saw these symptoms before. So, I asked the obvious question, what was wrong with Michael? What did she think was the problem? She just told me to take him to Children's Hospital. She went on to tell me that she wasn't allowed to tell me what was wrong or what she thought because she was not a doctor. After I questioned, I was like, "Everyone else has played the doctor role. Why not just tell me? Why put me through this? Why put Michael through this?" I remember when she said the condition, she thought he had, I just froze. Could it be that? Oh, my God. No, he couldn't have. All I knew about the condition was from what I saw on television. The words Muscular Dystrophy just repeated in my head over and over. It was like a song you could not get out of your head. It slowly played over and over. This started haunting me at the same time.

Michael's appointment was delayed until January 24, 2002. We arrived about an hour before his appointment. After we were called, we went into a small examination room. It didn't take too long before the doctor came in. I told Dr. S everything that was going on. His walking and falling was getting worse. Anything further than a block required the use of a stroller. So, he examined Michael and at first it was just the normal stuff, checked the heart, nose, and mouth. Then he asked Michael to sit on the floor and then asked him to get up. That is when his eyes rolled up and he looked worried. After that, he then excused himself and came back with Doctor M.

He asked Michael to sit down on the floor and get up. He looked more worried than the other doctor. Doctor M put his hand on his head and looked at me--then closed the door. Remember what I said about the truth? How do you want it, but really you don't at the same time? Well, this is one of many moments I felt like that. He said, "Michael has Duchenne's Muscular Dystrophy." I was in shock. The physical therapist was right. I saw these kids on television in wheelchairs with the Jerry guy. At that moment I told myself, perhaps this won't be so bad, A child in a wheelchair. He would have special needs, that's all. He would need some treatment.

So, I said it aloud, "When can he start treatment? He could get better. Right?" Doctor M, sat down next to me, he said very sadly, "Unfortunately there are no treatments and no cure at this time for Duchenne's Muscular Dystrophy, he will not get better, but just the opposite. He will lose his abilities starting with his lower body first and then the upper body. He will need a wheelchair. It will attack every muscle in the body, until." I looked at him, and slowly said,

"Until when?" He uttered the words, "It's terminal." No! No! No! It can't be terminal. I asked, "How long does he have?" The doctor, very compassionately said, "Everyone is different? He will most likely need a wheelchair by age ten and most boys lose their battle with the disease between the ages of 14-23. I am so sorry."

Later that day, Michael had a blood test to confirm the diagnosis. Within one hour the results came back with a CPK level of 15,000 which meant positive. All this time spent wondering what he had and all the doctors who just didn't know or didn't look hard enough, were finally answered. This was not just shocking, but unbelievable. All my dreams for Michael went out the window. I felt like a freight train dropped on me.

I was told about the MDA and to contact them. Honestly, at the hospital while the doctor was talking about what Michael had, I just blacked out. I completely withdrew and used a childhood coping strategy of flying away. The word terminal sounded more like this was the end. There was no cure, no hope, and no nothing. The doctors went on and on about all the other doctors that would be needed for his care. They spoke of the IEP for Michael that he would need and possibly a new school. A school that treats him like he is inferior and from another planet-- is no school for him. This will be confronted. I will be paying a visit to Chappell and to Lemoyne school to share this diagnosis with them. Chappell, who couldn't wait just a few weeks for the diagnosis, to place him correctly or should I say label him. Then, there is Lemoyne, who labeled and locked him in a little box, hidden from the world's view. They decided he could not be part of the normal world. The only one who showed kindness was the physical therapist who tried to help us find an answer to what was wrong with Michael.

## CHAPTER FIVE

## SHATTERED HOPES AND DREAMS

When I got home, I just cried and cried in disbelief that this was happening. I thought this was it. I better run to the store buy a bike, scooter, and skating board before it's too late. He only had so much time and nobody was sure exactly. We got the prognosis from all the doctors. Every time I thought of Michael's fate, I just started crying. When this happens you just feel helpless and hopeless. You are powerless. My faith was even being tested. How could God do this to Michael? Wasn't he one of God's children? Wasn't he supposed to love and protect him? At this point, I do not know if God and I are on good terms or not. Was I being punished for doing something? How was I going to tell Michael? I had to get it together because one day I would have to tell him. Then there was Ashley, how would I tell her? We would have to journey through this together. We had to take the good and the bad. I did contact his father to tell him the shocking news. He responded, "He didn't get it from my side of the family." Still the same jerk even with news like this. I needed some strength, but right now I feel drained.

I turned to writing music and short stories about what was going on with my son. I felt alone and so isolated from the world. My heart was shattered into a million pieces. I really didn't know if I was strong enough to handle this. I had to hide the fear, disappointment, and sadness that was ripping my heart apart. How could this be happening? This is such a mean disease. I have to gather strength and positive energy to fight this thing he has.

I had a few friends, Nessa, Jane, and Magic. Manny was a friend at work, but nothing more at this point. I kept my circle small. Nessa, I have spoken about. Jane was married to Andy, and they had a daughter named Anna. Jane had a son from her previous relationship, named Niko. He was a troubled child with a lot of issues. The stepfather had a challenging time being a father to Niko. I was Anna's Godmother. I didn't even know what even meant, but this was before I even had kids--so it sounded cool. Perhaps, that would make me part of a family.

Jane often leaned on me for support, so I thought she would be there for me. But she had so much drama in her life that she didn't have much time for me. My friends would run to tell me all their problems and expect me to listen. They wanted me to be their therapist and then fix their problems too. I really needed to make some new friends.

I also knew Jane's older brother, Tito, but I called him Uncle Tito. He was a producer for live shows. He was friends with Jesse and would hang out, per say. Jane would often complain that Tito was with Jesse doing some project. She sounded a bit jealous at times. I guess, typical sibling rivalry. Then there were other times, she would tell me about the live shows in which her brother met many famous people. She would name all of them to me and I could have taken it as bragging, but she just sounded so proud of him. I would talk to him often and he was always supportive-- motivating. He was impartial, even know I was his sister's friend.

Magic was different, he offered more than I would take. I have known him since I was a kid in foster care. He lived far from me in California. I really needed someone to be there for me. So, after calling Jane and Nessa I decided to call Magic. I felt pushed aside and like they didn't even care. So, when I called him, he could hear in my voice that something was wrong. When I uttered the words of the condition, there was a silence before he said something to me. He told me, "No, he could have that." Then when I confirmed it, I just lost it and started to cry. He was supportive over the phone. He said that I shouldn't be alone and insisted I come to California with the kids. He begged me to come because he really wanted to be there for me. He even offered to come to Chicago to get me, pay the rent and anything else I needed. This was an emotional time and I really needed someone at this point to be there for me. I hesitated at first, but then decided to go. It was a suitable time to go, I was given permission to use my vacation time due to the circumstances. My college even allowed me to miss, just as long as I emailed all my papers to my professors. There weren't any tests that I would miss. So, I left a few days later. Magic took care of everything. He had a big house off the coast, and it was beautiful. I can't wait to see Magic.

After arriving in California, Magic picked me up. We drove back to the house and the kids slept the entire way. We spent a lot of time with the children on the beach. I broke down that night in the living room right in front of the piano. I really felt that I had done something to make God upset. But Magic didn't believe that and just held me in his arms to comfort me. He was sweet to me and even insisted that I moved to California with him. But I resisted by saying, I have a life in Chicago. I even contemplated before giving my definitive answer. Part of me thought of taking the effortless way out, however the other part-- kept saying no. I wanted to do this on my own. I know he could give me the world, but I wasn't ready for his world yet. Magic was an artist and writer, so he was busy. But maybe one day, I will be ready to be in another relationship, which is what he wished for. He wanted more than I could give at this point, but he didn't abandon me. He now wanted me to come during Spring break and I agreed with him. We spent a lot of time together and he was a great comfort.

After leaving, I started missing him a lot. I knew I loved him as a friend. but I had so much happened. I didn't want him to feel any burden and I had said that to him before, so he insisted that wasn't true. So, he would call every night and we would talk. On Sundays, we would talk for hours while I would type my papers. He would even send letters. He even sent money a few times, but I told him to stop because it made me feel uncomfortable taking his money. So, then he started sending gifts to the kids and me--which was the same as with the money. He was generous like that, but he honored my wishes--except on birthdays.

At night while lying in bed, I was trapped with my thoughts about Ashley and Michael. I couldn't tell Magic how bad I was feeling. I felt like I was deceiving him, but I didn't want him to feel bad. Also, all of this was hard for me to cope with. It was tough for magic as well. He wanted me to move to California and we had many conversations about this. I love Chicago! I couldn't believe over the years what people said, "I was lucky that I did not have an active boy jumping all over the place." I would see my friend's struggle with their boys. I didn't like the fact that they made it look like all the boys were hyperactive and the girls were perfect. They put them into these boxes of what is normal or not.

The truth is--you worry when the kid is not active. All kids are meant to have all this energy. You should be happy to see your kid run around the house like an endless energizer battery. When they don't have all this energy, that is when to call the doctor and demand answers. But even then, the doctors just give you a sugarcoated answer and just dismiss your concerns. That's until it gets to a point where it becomes too obvious you can't ignore. How could they not have seen this? I do blame his primary doctor, at least for now because he always blamed that fact that he was a boy. What did that have to do with anything? Now, my baby Michael will suffer. I hope that he has been blessed with my strength and spirit because he's going to need it.

CHAPTER SIX

# MDA World

In May 2002, I took Michael for his first visit at the MDA. We met doctors at Rush Medical Center. Dr. Peters and Dr. Son have been with the MDA for over 20 years. Michael was given a case manager who arranged all his appointments. At this point he would come here every 6 months and see everyone in one place. He would see the Neurologist, Cardiologist, Pulmonologist, Orthopedic specialist, Physical therapist (PT) and Occupational therapist (OT). They told me the same as the other doctors told me at Children's Hospital about Michael's condition and what to expect. I was hoping that Michael would have until age 10 and not be confined to a wheelchair. They gave us a book, called Journey's A Guide for Parents with a Child with Duchenne's Muscular Dystrophy known better as DMD. I was told to apply for SSI for Michael and that he qualifies due to having DMD. We were told about the MDA camp that would be fun for him to meet other kids with the condition. It was an away camp for an entire week in which he would be with a volunteer counselor who would take care of him. Michael smiled when I told him about the camp, so I guess I will let him go. It was a lot of information and just so overwhelming. In just a matter of a short few months Michael and our lives changed forever and kept on doing so.

Michael was having issues with getting on the bus to school. He lost the ability to walk up and down stairs. The bus attendant said she could not assist him. I contacted the school and had to fight with them about having someone assist him on and off the bus. They wouldn't allow a parent or babysitter to do it. They gave me a lot of excuses and in the end, they claimed they did not know he had Muscular Dystrophy. I told them so many times and even gave them the doctor's letters. They were being difficult and trying to make people, like ourselves, jump through hula hoops. This is the red tape that creates roadblocks which is unfair. I was so glad he was not going to be at this school next year.

In June 2002, Michael went to the MDA camp and had so much fun. It gave me a chance to spend time with Ashley, who for the most part had no idea what was going on. She just turned two and nothing seemed out of place yet. Ashley was going to start preschool. Everything in her world was normal and nothing was shaken yet. He came home all happy but then came the questions. He said that an older child at the camp said, "His brother died from what I have." He added, "Kids die from this condition." I just froze and I didn't know what to say to him. That book they gave me had nothing in there about talking to him about this. Why didn't kids come with a book of directions?

Michael asked, "What is wrong with me? Am I going to die?" Oh, boy-- it is questions like this that make you go into overload. Michael didn't know what death means. I didn't know what to say. I slowly... said, "Well Michael, you have a disease Duchenne's Muscular Dystrophy. And one day, none of us will be here." I thought that might be enough for him. Michael knew too much already. He insisted that he heard the name of the disease at the camp and people die from it. He associated the word "die," with he won't see me anymore--not the adult term. But he was right, he wouldn't see me anymore. He said, "You don't have to tell me, I know it makes you sad. It makes me sad, too. I don't want to leave you." I just hugged him and said, "We don't have to talk about this. We are together right now. I love you so much." He slowly waddled away.

In late June, I was approved for the Low-Income Housing Program which allowed me to have a bigger place and the rent was based on my income. Finally, I can get a break here. I found out my rent would only be $157 a month. This was a blessing. We moved to another place on the North side of Chicago-- near Peterson. It was a two-bedroom apartment. It was nice and spacious for the children. I barely had anything in the apartment. The kids' room had bunkbeds and I fixed it up nicely. My room had a bed, a desk, and a television.

There was another television in the living room--which I bought with my tax return. I was able to afford a microwave and a few other new things.

The only problem is the apartment was on the third floor. Michael had already lost his ability to walk up and down the stairs, so I would have to carry him. Walking in general was slow and he looked like he was about to fall. He needed a walker now and I was waiting for the insurance to approve it. The kids loved the apartment. We were safer here, away from their father knowing where we were. We were in a constant fight with the insurance company and the school. It appears insurances and schools are not equal for all.

In August, Nessa arrived back in Chicago with Jonas, so she came to stay at my new place. She loved it. All the kids were in one room. Nessa and I shared a room. She enrolled for classes at Wright College with me again. She said that she was staying for good this time. Next year, she was going to bring her older daughter Kate to live here with us. Jonas was enrolled with Ashley for school at the YMCA. I went to school in the morning and worked in the evening. The kids were at the preschool-daycare until 6pm. Then Junior would watch the kids until I came home. Then he would go pick up Nessa from school, around 9pm. Junior spent a lot of time at my house. He worked overnights at some company near Lane Tech High School. So, it all worked out.

CHAPTER SEVEN

# HIDDEN DISCRIMINATIONS

Every year on Labor Day, there was an MDA Telethon that was aired on television. Jerry Lewis hosted it every year. Kids were referred to as, "Jerry's Kids." During the telethon, celebrities would talk about the many forms of muscular dystrophies and the effects. In addition, there would be performances and other forms of entertainment. They would try to raise as much money as they could to help individuals and families living with MD. This disease didn't only affect children, but adults as well. The money raised was used for research, treatments, MDA camps, and equipment--such as wheelchairs and walkers. The telethon didn't only educate, but it always gave people hope.

In September 2002, Michael was to start school at Hayat Grade School. I was working and going to school, which was hard, but I felt something was going to get better. After I finish school, I will get a much better job. I got a call on the first day of school, that Michael wouldn't be allowed to attend school because the driver did not want to take him to school with the walker. The school decided that Michael should be in a wheelchair for transport. This turned into a big ordeal; that would allow transportation to have the power to refuse Michael to gain entry to the school unless he was in a wheelchair. I currently don't have a wheelchair for Michael. I had to get a loaner from the MDA. This took time and the doctors warned me that this action would cause Michael to weaken more. I know it might sound crazy, and you would think if he rested in a wheelchair, that when he needed to walk, he would have more energy, not so. There is a phase in the MD family, "If you do not use it, you will lose it." So, the more he was in a stroller or a wheelchair, the weaker he would become. Furthermore, the MDA said that this was discrimination and a violation of his rights. And if they continued down this road, I had the right to sue the school district. All of this was a violation of the Persons with Disability Act, 1974.

At the end of October 2002, after weeks of fighting with the school, Michael was put in a wheelchair for transport. This was one of the biggest mistakes that was made. I also had trouble at work, I had to change my schedule around, so that I would be home to get Michael off the bus and carry him up the three flights of stairs to the babysitter waiting. Then I had to rush back to work or school depending on what day it was. The kids were well behaved though, Ashley loved school, but Michael I was not so sure. He didn't say much about school. Something seemed off about his new school.

In Early December 2002, Michael came home from school complaining that his head hurt. He was acting out of it. I didn't understand what was wrong with him. I took him to the hospital thinking that it was part of his condition. Michael admitted when we got to the hospital that night that he had fallen twice at the school and hit his head. It turned out that Michael had a concussion. I was furious with the school because they never told me anything. There was no incident report and no call home from the school. Why do they think they can do this to Michael? Did they think I would not find out? Did they think he didn't matter, and he wouldn't tell? The problem is that most kids don't tell. This is outrageous and the school is going to be confronted. I intend on taking it to the school district if I must. I want him out of this school and to go to Solomon Grade School. I was told that Solomon is a great school when it comes to working with kids with disabilities. This school has no idea how to instruct kids with special needs.

Christmas 2002, Michael, and Ashley were excited about the gifts they received. This was the first Christmas at the new house. They were very appreciative of everything they got. They were never spoiled or ever complained about what they received. They never asked me for anything, either. I never got the tantrums in the store like some of the other parents. They really are exceptional children, but I worry about Ashley all the time. How will this affect her with Michael having MD? How does a terminal illness affect the other child in the house? At the same time, how does it affect the parents or parent? Unexpectedly, Alex recently suggested we get back together to have another baby since we would lose Michael. Wow, was that his way of saying he feels guilty? Thanks, but no thanks Alex. I could not believe he would say such a thing to me. I think sometimes people do not know what to say, so they say the first thing that comes to mind which usually is not the wisest. He did more disappearing acts on the children. Perhaps once a year he would just show up and say the most annoying things. At least now days he doesn't try to hurt me.

I was really stressed with all the things going on in my life. Being a parent of a child who has a special condition and a school that did not allow him to be treated like all the other children was wrong. Things start to take a toll. Then there was sweet little Ashley who did not know what was going on. Going to college full time and working was hard enough without all the drama with Michael. I just wanted him to be treated fairly. He deserved the same access to an education. I was overloaded and needed some release from all this pressure. I made a complaint to the school about what they were doing to Michael. I finally got a call that there was going to be an investigation and see if Michael had been discriminated from school based on his disability. At night, I would talk to Nessa about all these issues going on. She understood and was supportive. She was even coming to the meeting at the school.

## CHAPTER EIGHT

# THE FIGHT FOR MICHAEL AND BEYOND

In January, I had a meeting at the school concerning issues of Michael being at the school. I was given a tour of his room, and what I saw was shocking. Michael was in a self-contained room. This was just an educational term, which was at least for Michael, that he is a waste of time teaching. When we all know at the end what is going to happen. Again, the school just locked Michael away and just made these decisions based on what? Physical special needs do not dictate intelligence. Some people, especially the school system, love to connect that physical special needs equates lower intelligence. Furthermore, with anything that arises with his health--they just blame it on Muscular Dystrophy. According to the school, everything must make sense, so they try to group everything together, even when the puzzle pieces do not match. We must blame one disease and all the subtitles must fall right into the same category. We never want to think too hard and overanalyze it when it could be something totally unrelated going on.

Michael did not need this kind of room. It was unfair and it was discrimination. I demanded for Michael to be removed from the room, but they refused. I requested a new IEP. Again, they refused and claimed they had no time. How can they do this to Michael? How can they treat him like this? They were making all the decisions against my wishes. Who protects Michael from such discriminatory measures? By placing a title on him and his disabilities, they could ignore his truly gifted abilities. It is time to make a formal complaint to the Board of Education. They will listen to me. I will have to fight for Michael.

I spent the rest of the school year fighting with the school about a better placement for Michael. I was either given the run around that usually ended in a roadblock or I was just ignored altogether. It was just an awful feeling to be powerless in a situation. I cried about it and then prayed on top of that-- which led to more tears. I felt bad for Michael. He wanted to learn other things at his level but was being given a non-verbal education with coloring sheets. Something has to give. I really needed to see light at the end of the tunnel.

In April, I had a meeting at the school. Nessa came with me for support. They thought that Nessa was my romantic partner-- not just a friend. I thought that was kind of funny that the school took the time to analyze my living situation instead of doing their job; to analyze what is a better way to educate Michael rather than discriminating against him. They got this information from the psychologist who did the evaluation for this meeting. I sat down with this so-called psychologist, and she took the information I gave her, so she could draft her report. During the entire meeting she kept saying, "I get it and understand." What did she understand? She certainly didn't get it either. So, I wasn't looking forward to seeing her or most of the people at the school who made the decisions they made. Michael was out of school for a few months and the only way to come back was to put him in a wheelchair which was not in the best interest of Michael.

So, I was shocked when I walked into a room, and around the table were complete strangers. The psychologists, the social workers, his teacher, and the vice principal were all fired. There was a school official from the Chicago School Board. I thought I was going to have to fight with these people, but everyone went around and introduced themselves. They were nice. At the end, the School Board official stated that Michael's was discriminated based on disability. Due to this finding, he was here at the meeting--not only apologize, but ensure Michael is placed in the most appropriate school. I was asked where I wanted Michael to go to school and if I had done any research.

I told him that I wanted Michael to be at Solomon. My request was granted with busing. I was so happy. The school district settled out of court for an undisclosed amount paid to me--on Michael's behalf.

A couple of weeks later, I received a call from Michael's teacher, Ms. Clark. I was concerned when I got the call. But the teacher was so nice and stated that Michael was a very smart child. She insisted that I had the right to order a new IEP to be done on Michael. In addition, she stated that the way this IEP was written --Michael would be in a self-contained room, and he was smarter than that. I agreed to come to the school to sign the papers to get the ball rolling.

Ashley was denied the right to go to school with her brother.

There are rules to education that really cause hardship for families. Both of the kids were not only subjected to a pattern of discrimination based on physical abilities which I will refer to as being able-bodied; they were subjected to racial discrimination and the fact I was a single parent. I was seen as white, and the children were seen as Black. Many white people have trouble seeing beyond the color to see the features that are visibly there. I clearly was not "just white, "but the school staff would make comments. How race, ethnicity, and color are defined in America does not seem to be in agreement and often knocks children into the "other" category. It's the people in power who get to make and revise what being white means. There is a very subjective definition of what white means. The rules of race have been getting challenged since the first bi-racial babies were born. They too, got some names. There were very biased and racist comments sometimes, said right in front of me. Ignorant people with ignorant thinking cause prejudices that lead to discrimination and oppression, with excuses made by the oppressors to make sense of their own behaviors.

Since my foster care days, I saw discrimination against foster children and on a racial level. There were labels given that allowed foster parents and staff to verbally abuse children of color. This behavior was disgusting and left a nasty stain in my mind of what the department allowed. But we will revisit this conversation about race, discrimination, and labels. My daughter Ashley would face some of the harshest racial discrimination. People often judge what they don't or refuse to understand. A lot of people like to force people into boxes with specific labels which do not feel good at all. As the school year started to wind down, I had a meeting at the school the first week of June. At the meeting I got to hear positive things said about Michael and realistic goals were set. Overall, Michael was said to only have a PH need and nothing more. His intelligence was normal, and he did not have a learning disability. Next year, he was to be placed in a regular classroom--not special education. This was a win for Michael.

In June, Michael celebrated his birthday. We had a small party with cake and ice cream. Michael would not eat the cake. He did not like sweets at all. He always refused it and would rather have fish, rice, and hot sauce. He must have gotten that from his father. His father loved hot food and I think it is part of his ethnicity. Michael visited the MDA clinic, and it was always the same unwelcome news, "He's getting worse." That phrase is hard to hear every time. Then the issue of Michael using the wheelchair for transport was wrong, so the social worker and the doctors told me. It was the same as I was already told before--that it was discrimination.

Michael was losing the ability to walk fast. Ashley would now pull him on his feet to get him around the house. I thought it looked awful, but Michael said it was fun. Then the other times, Michael would crawl to get from one place to another. So, this was the beginning of the end for Michael to walk. How do I tell him that he is losing that ability? Something that was taken for granted by so many people was now going to pass him by like it never existed. There were no medications to stop or cure the disease. There was a drug called prednisone that perhaps can slow down the progression of the disease. It was suggested that Michael should take it on an everyday basis. So, I decided to give it a shot.

The summer 2003, Michael went to the MDA camp like every year. This camp allowed him to get away from all the medical stuff and fly away from the disease for one week. He always enjoyed it and came back very tired from the long week full of activities and fun. Ashley went to the camp at the YMCA for the entire summer and had a blast. This summer Ashley was seen doing gymnastics. The coach thought she was good and strong for her age, so he encouraged her to join the gymnastics program at the YMCA. He told me about the team for the girls. So, I thought about it and let her take the lessons. She got a scholarship, and we did not have to pay. I could not have afforded the prices either. She really enjoyed gymnastics. At least she can escape Michael being sick while being at the gym.

Most of the focus was on Michael and his health, which took away time from Ashley. In the beginning, she was young and had to just go along with her vibes as to how she was feeling. Later, she would talk about things relating to being at the hospital and other medical visits with Mike. I tried to shield her from all this medical stuff going on with her brother. Gymnastics became her escape for the most part, but questions came up here and there. They were answered at her age level. I was sure that we would revisit these questions at some point.

Ashley had some behavioral issues at school from time to time. These issues were always brought up like it was the end of the world. They were almost always blamed on the fact that I was a single mother with her race being tied into the conversation. I never thought that race issues would come up in preschool, but I was wrong. First, there were these beautiful Nigerian girls in her class named Imani and Imelli. Ashley had a Black doll and the girls told her that she should play with a white doll. I understood the girls and their mother only saw me pick her up and they never saw her father. They never would either, for reasons already explained. Ashley came out of school a few times and told me what the girls had told her about the doll playing. I explained to her the girls are wrong and she can play with any color dolls. I always brought her all color/ethnicity dolls—white, brown, Black, Asian, and Native American. I wanted her to embrace all of who she is and for her to choose the doll she assimilates to. Well, she was being judged. I could not believe what happened next.

The girl's mother confronted me, and she told me that my daughter should only play with white dolls. I do not know why I entertained the idea in the first place, but I was young and caught off guard. So, it went something like this, she attacked me with her words. She almost gasped when I told her that her father was from Liberia. Her mouth just dropped, then she looked at my daughter. She then said, "No, our men do not mess with light-skinned women."

She continued, "Well, she is not Black." She then walked out.

The next day, Ashley became the spectacle by the same girl's grandmother, their father, and another Nigerian mother of what my daughter was. The grandmother of the girls was the wisest, she said, "Well, she has the distinctive features, but looks a bit Asian." She smiled at my daughter, and said, "She is beautiful, and her color will come later." She handed my daughter a Nigerian homemade doll and walked away. There was a very unwelcoming stare and feeling the mother and her friend gave me for the rest of the time while Ashley attended. Another incident that took place at the school came when Ashley had braids. These same girls threw sand and paint in her hair. Ashley threw the sand back at them, and while she was doing this— sand got into another girl's braids, named Jasmine. The grandmother of this other girl got all up in Nessa's face and ordered her to pay for the braids. Nessa refused and informed the grandmother that it was the two other girls that started the sand/paint fight. We later found out that the girl's mother told them to do that to my daughter. I was amazed how the issue was dropped as soon as the grandmother found out my daughter did not start situation. The treatment my daughter and the fact that she was constantly being asked, "What are you? Where did you come from? Are you adopted?" These questions would follow her for many years to come.

In July 2003, we moved from the third floor to the basement apartment with two bedrooms. It was nice to be closer to the ground with Michael. I would have to carry him up and then bring up his wheelchair. It was challenging work, but it had to be done. But now we were on the ground floor, which made life in that regard a little easier. Michael started asking questions, "Why he was in a wheelchair?" So, I told him that he had neuromuscular progressive disease called Duchenne's Muscular Dystrophy. Every time I had to say the name of his condition--I felt great heartache. This is something, as a mother, nobody really can understand--unless they have had a child with a terminal illness. Nobody knows otherwise.

In September 2003, Michael went back to Solomon Grade school and Ashley was at the still YMCA. Solomon grade school did offer pre-k, but still would not allow Ashley to attend. I was hoping for kindergarten she would be able to join her brother. Michael was finally, where he needed to be school wise, so I felt a little more at peace and a lot calmer. Nessa helped a lot too. Junior basically lives with us now but would help take care of the kids while Nessa and I were out. Junior was a good father to his son and my kids as well.

# CHAPTER NINE

## FULL PLATES OF NORMAL

Everyone was busy at the house. Between working and school, I did not have too much time for anything else, except for being a parent, which was a full-time job. Nessa and Junior got back together as a couple. They did have some attraction between them which was nice to see. Junior liked to curse a lot, so I had to constantly say something to him about that because the kids would pick it up, I feared. We all had schedules that went around the children, so that they would all be taken care of. Everything seemed to work out.

Michael was never treated any differently in the house from the other kids. I never told him he could not, so he never thought that. Michael was a good, spirited child with no harsh feeling towards anyone because he had this condition. He was not bitter in any way either. He had this big smile that lit up a room and those eyes, oh my goodness. I was happy that he had my smile, Brighteyes, spirit and strength. Many people, especially when I went to the school, knew right away I was Michael's mother because he had these qualities I mentioned. Even the people who didn't know me and just met me for the first time, knew this.

Michael never once complained about anything ever hurting him. He would always say, "Mommy I'm okay--I love you." He was sweet like that. But no matter how much you try to ignore it--Michael's disease was there. I always tried to refer to his disease as a condition--only because it gave me more hope. Disease to me, meant terminal-end—complete, and no more. Condition meant hope, possibilities, and life. I tried to block out of my head everyday what was to come and his real prognosis. He was put on Prednisone to slow down this relentless disease. The side effects were just awful. All of this would take a toll on me. Just to think of it make me sad and I would often cry at night. It can test even the strongest character and moral beliefs.

I tried to keep my sad feelings away from Michael and Ashley. I did this out of compassion and love for them being able to live a normal childhood. This was something I was never given the opportunity to enjoy. I wanted to give them the stability and love I was never given. Being a foster child changes your views on family. Sometimes it can make you the best parent you can be, but on the other hand, it can lead to you being the worst. I know the alternative to parents who become the worst--the foster care system. I decided before I had children that I would never let my children go through what I did. For the most part, I succeeded. But I wanted them to have more, so I went to college to make that happen.

I worked hard in college and employment wise. I had trouble keeping hours at my job with my current availability due to Michael's needs. Nessa and Junior played lovebirds at the house. Nessa was jealous and always thought that he was out cheating on her. She was so suspicious that she would even make up stories about him cheating--just so she could feel that she was right. Junior had a little girl, named Amy who would come to the house. I later found out she was a runaway when the police came by my house. She turned out to be 14 years old and had no business here. She was not from a troubled home, but she just liked to be a rebel and stay out. She showed up again at my house soon after the police took her back home. She sat in my kitchen telling me about the world and complaining. She said that going to college was a waste of time and she knew that I was stressed out. So, she continued with her juvenile comments, that I should just quit and get my own place. That is a bit much from a child who already was skipping classes and ran away to hang out with Junior. I did inform her this was my apartment not Junior's or Nessa's. She seemed to have things confused. I did not see her too much after that.

All this stuff was stressful and a bit of a distraction from everything else going on. I allowed Nessa and Junior to be at my house, mainly because I had no family. So, they were like family. I was hoping soon they would perhaps move out together with son and daughter. Kate, who is 10 years old, has shoulder length mahogany brown hair, and a very thick body type came from Florida just a few weeks after school started. She attended Michael's old school before he was transferred. There was a school just down the street, but it was a magnet school where you must apply to get in. So, Kate had to walk twelve blocks to school. She had some issues, which included some behavioral problems, but overall, she was reacting to her parents' living situation. Kate was confused about living in Florida with her grandparents. She gave me a tough time in the beginning, but after a while she started behaving. Her mother said that she had ADHD, and she was on medication. Other than that--she seemed well adjusted after the move, except for using the N-word against my children. This word she had picked up from her grandparents, but she was in Chicago now. She will create a race war at her new school if she does not stop using that word.

During the Holidays 2003, we all spent time together making dinner and all that. We all put our money together to make Christmas great for the kids. There seemed to be a great battle between Nessa being here in Chicago and her family in Florida. This often-upset Junior who just wanted to spend time with his children. I observed the situation but tried to stay out of their business. They were the parents of their children, so I gave them that respect--unless they asked. The kids all got along for the most part. Michael and Jonas got along like brothers, but Michael got along with everyone. He just had that great personality like that. He was a charmer with that great smile.

Magic would call every night and would send several letters a week. He always sent sweet letters that were always very thoughtful and caring. He still wanted me to move to California and I was thinking about it more and more. I really wanted someone to be closer in distance that would be there for me. I needed to be loved and held at times too. He would send inspiring cards that always came with a check or two. I would call him to thank him, but as soon as I said that I did not want to take his money--he would change the subject. So, I kind of just stopped fighting with him on that. I insisted that it was only a loan until I finished school. He would always respond, "Yes, whatever you say." He was worried about the people I was living with because they did not sound anything like me. He was right, they really were not. They were rough around the edges--that is all. He was being very persistent about me moving there, and I did consider it. He was trying to wear me down a bit. Maybe one day—I will give in.

## CHAPTER TEN

# MAKING GREAT MEMORIES AND WISHES

In March 2004, Michael was granted a wish from Make-a-Wish Foundation. His wish was to go to Disney World! So, we decided to go the first week of June--which was his birthday. I called Magic to tell him the great news and as usual he was so excited. Nessa decided when we went to Disney that she was taking the kids to Florida for a week. The kids were so excited to go, but Junior felt it was unfair that his kids were not included in the wish. I understood because this trip was awfully expensive that it can only include immediate family and one extra adult. As the trip came closer to us leaving, I started to pack. I invited Manny, a friend from work, to come along. Junior was going to stay at a friend's house for the week while we were gone.

In May, Ashley graduated from pre-school and would start kindergarten in the Fall. She would not be able to go to school with her brother and this created a conflict, once again. She was being sent to another school in the completely opposite direction, which would create hardship for me in getting her there with no school bus transportation. There was no sense in doing this, so I protested and would be granted a meeting in late September. I was happy for her to leave the preschool she was attending, but her new school-- Trumbull Elementary was not close by any means. Over the summer, she would attend a gymnastics camp. Ashley was excited about that, but not happy she could not attend school with her brother in the

Fall. Michael would have a busy summer, first with the Make a Wish trip and second with the MDA camp.

I left for the trip with the kids and Manny at 6am. The limo was nice, and the kids were so excited about getting to Disney World. Nessa left an hour after for Miami. We would be in Orlando which was further up North. We arrived in Florida at 11am and a man was there to pick us up. His name was Rich, and he was more of a guide. He was from "Give Kids the World Village." Well, let me explain, most of the families stay in the village, but some families stay at hotels in the Walt Disney resort. We were going to stay at the Polynesian Hotel, which was nice. We had a rental car waiting so Rich walked us through everything, which was nice. We loaded the car and headed to the hotel. Not being from this area, it took us some time to get there.

As we pulled into the hotel parking lot--the scenery was so beautiful. I could see the hotel from afar and it was so big. Two men came out to help us up to our room. They unloaded the car and we walked ahead. Michael and Ashley's eyes were so wide with amazement. As we entered the hotel--it was like we entered another world. There was a waterfall inside the hotel with palm trees. The atmosphere just gave the feeling of complete calmness. The architecture was so beautiful that it was breathtaking. As we walked on the path to the hotel room which was surrounded by these beautiful palm trees, and I saw the most beautiful sky. Then I looked over past a large tree and I was amazed at what I saw. It looked like Magic was standing there. I had to look twice out of disbelief. I continued walking to the hotel thinking, perhaps I was tired.

The room was just as beautiful as the hotel. It was Hawaiian themed which was so beautiful. I always wanted to go to Hawaii, so this might be the closest I can get, for now at least. We unpacked a little, but the kids wanted to get to the pool and water slide. We had a magnificent view of the entire water park from the balcony. So, I quickly got dressed and then helped Ashley. Manny help Michael and we headed to the pool. The bright sun was shining on my face and the blue sky was so bright. The pool was like a beach and the big water slide was so nice. The area was surrounded again by these beautiful palm trees. The architecture of the Hawaiian theme was so evident all over the resort. There was a beach about one thousand feet from the pools.

I took Ashley over there. She had never seen a real beach with white sand and clear blue water. This was a beach--not like Lake Michigan in Chicago. I love beaches because they make me feel such calmness and peace that circulates all through my body. After all this stress, being here was amazing. I may never get another opportunity like this for a while, so I better take advantage of it. Ashley enjoyed her time at the beach and had a smile ear to ear. We stayed at the beach for a few hours, until the kids were a bit hungry.

Tomorrow we will take the monorail to the Magic Kingdom, then Epcot, MGM, Animal Kingdom, Sea World, and Universal Studios. The hotel was paid for, and I was given the keys to the hotel room. I received the cards for all the attractions-no charge to us. A gift card with a generous amount of spending money and money for meals was also given. So basically, everything was taken care of. Michael will never forget this trip. So, I went to get the kids some pizza before they got too tired. As I was heading to the pizza place, I saw Magic right in front of me. He ran over to give me a hug. I was so amazed that he was here. He flew all the way to see me. He invited me to have coffee after the little ones went to sleep. He was even staying at the same hotel. So, I took the pizza to the children, and we all ate. Afterwards, the kids took baths and went to bed. Manny went to sleep on the daybed. I went for a walk and met up with Magic for some coffee. We went to a lounge and sat down to talk on the second floor. We talked for about three hours before I went back to my room. He really did not want me to go, but I was tired. He said before leaving, "I love you." I smiled, and said, "I love you too." I gave him a hug and waved bye.

Early in the morning, we left for the Magic Kingdom. Michael and Ashley were wearing their Make-a-Wish shirts with their tags around their necks. These tags would allow them to go to the front of the lines for all the rides, exhibits and to take pictures with their favorite characters. I also had the tags to wear as mommy. These kids had it made because all the other guests had to pay for the luxury of not waiting in line. Mine got it for free. The kids went from ride to ride the entire day. They did not want to stop and eat. I had to make them drink something because it was so hot. But these kids just wanted to go-go-go. They had a blast. I had a couple favorite rides they became the kids favorite too--the Haunted Mansion and It's a Small World After all. I wish I could build these rides behind my house. Maybe someday.

Manny was moving so fast from ride to ride, that he forgot to buckle Michael's wheelchair seatbelt. As a result, Michael fell out and hit his head on the pavement. He was checked by a nurse at the first aid clinic, and she told us that he seemed fine. He did have a rather hard head. So, we continued on to have more fun, and went on all the rides--like three times. Ashley was asked if she wanted to ride on one of the floats for the parade. She said, "Yes, of course." It was such an exciting moment for her to be part of this magic. She was dressed as Cinderella. The night ended with the most magnificent fireworks show that they had ever seen. It was so magical for them to see this for the first time, and they lit up with such excitement. I had seen it before, but I have to say, it was just as exciting as when I first saw it as a young child.

The next day was Michael's birthday. We went to Give the Kids the World Village. They gave him a cake and a special picture with all the Disney friends. Then we headed off to Animal Kingdom where we went on the water raft ride about seven times. Then I saw the life tree which was beautiful. Then we went on all the other rides until the park closed. Over the next few days, we went to all the other parks. But, by the time we got to Universal Studios--the weather started getting a little scary. There was lightning, so most of the day the rides had to be closed. Instead, we did a lot of sightseeing and ate at some exciting places. Over the week, I saw Magic every day for coffee. He told me that next year he wanted me to join him on a cruise with the children. He wanted an answer, but I told him that I would let him know depending on the dates. He then decided to ask me for the dates that I could go, and he would make all the arrangements. So, I just smiled and agreed. He left that night, and we left the next morning.

I was exhausted from the trip, and I think the kids were as well. Manny was so tired but thanked me for inviting him along. When I got to the airport in Chicago, I called home because I knew Nessa was already there. Kate answered the phone and was rude to me. Nessa took the phone from her and asked when we would be home. I let her know we were on our way. It was a long ride home with the kids and I carried Michael from the car. Manny carried little Ashley inside and then got back to the limo. The driver agreed to drop him at his house. I put the kids to bed and started to unpack. When I went into my room, I noticed it smelled bad and there was food and some other disgusting things on the wall. When I walked in the living room, there was nasty stuff all over the carpet. The house looked totally trashed--like there were people in my house the entire week.

So, just then Nessa and Junior came in as the doting couple. They came in with clean laundry. I asked her what happened here. She then told me that she gave the keys to Junior, and he stayed here the entire week while we were gone. She said that he had some people over. So, she did not really know what happened. Junior told me that he was sorry. I was not happy about this--not at all. I trusted them and they did this. Then I started to see something I had not seen before. They had taken over my house with their kids. Neighbors would come to the house asking for Junior and even commenting that it was nice that they were letting me stay here with my kids. I thought, really? This is my apartment, and it is quite the opposite. This was not right. Junior nor Nessa was working. I started to feel used. Nessa and Junior got in a big fight and Junior went to live at one of his father's buildings. They would have fights like this all the time. Oh, wonder Kate acted the way she did. The girl was confused. Things were quiet after that. Nessa seemed more focused with him being gone.

## CHAPTER ELEVEN

# New Beginnings

Michael went to the MDA summer camp in July 2004. Michael's volunteer counselor was Megan. She was tall, skinny and had brown hair. She was around age sixteen and lived in the North Suburbs near Chicago. She was nice to Michael and was so excited. She did seem a little hyper, but that was good positive energy for Michael. So, I left him in good hands. While he was at the summer camp, I moved across the way to another basement apartment. This time it was a three-bedroom. So, the boys had a separate room from the girls. Then I had my own room. Nessa took the living room. So, Junior came to help us move, but did not say much to Nessa. We set up the entire house within a few days and before I had to pick up Michael. So, I am always happy to pick up Michael, but this is also a sad day for him because he always has such an enjoyable time which makes saying goodbye so hard. Megan asked to keep in contact with Michael, so I gave our number to her. Michael said he had a lot of fun with Megan all week. He talked so much about the camp, that he fell asleep on the way home. After arriving home, Michael was so excited to see the new apartment. As I walked in, Nessa was having a fight with Junior which caused him to leave as soon as I walked in with Mike.

On Sundays, the kids all went to a church In Hamond, Indiana. I worked all day Sunday, so it was a nice break for Nessa. She cleaned the house on Sundays when everyone was gone but was all about Junior when he was at the house. They really needed to get a place of their own. This break-up will not last too long. Ashley started to act up, most likely as a response into all the fighting between Junior and Nessa. In addition, Kate started yelling and throwing loud tantrums. Mainly, Kate wanted attention from her parents, but was not getting it. Nessa was right there in front of her daughter and still ignored her. Junior was no longer living in the home. I would be at home at night now because I would only work four days a week--Thursday through Sunday. I had classes only on Monday-Tuesday-Wednesday from 7am-4pm. The kids were well behaved when I would take care of them. Even Kate would behave for me. Her parent's issues were making her act crazy. I didn't know how much more I could take of this.

Megan kept her promise and called to pick Michael up for the day. So, she took Michael out to lunch and some other fun activities. She would do this almost every week. As the start date for school approached, I was trying to get the kids ready with all the normal stuff. I had to take Michael to get shoes and some uniforms. Megan called and really wanted to pick him up, but I could not let her because I had things to do with Mike. She became persistent and even offered to take Michael to get shoes. I really did not like other people doing for Michael. I really did not know her or her family well, but in the end, I just let him go. I told her not to buy him the shoes and she agreed. I did not feel comfortable allowing that.

After she brought Michael home, she handed me an envelope and told me that it was from her dad. After she left, I looked in it and it was full of money. I was really confused, so I called her later to ask her about the money. She said that it was from her dad and to have fun with it. I was like, ok--well thank you. It still did not make sense, but ok. Later that night, I was putting Michael to bed and noticed he was wearing new shoes. It was nice that she went out to buy him new shoes, but I asked her not to. I just did not want this to become a thing because I did not want any issues. I am used to doing things on my own because then you do not owe anyone. Perhaps now I am struggling, but one day I will be done with college and will not be. I did not understand why this family wanted to help. What was the exchange? I do not just trust people like that. Most people want something in return. Even my friend Magic wanted something in return. It was not anything materialistic, but it was companionship, love, and a family. What did they want? The next weekend, Megan's father, Peter came to drop off Michael after he went to their house for the day. Michael always would come home and tell me about their big house with a pool in the back. Then he would turn to me and say, "Can we have a house like them?" I did not say anything to my son with big eyes. Peter looked around as we talked a while, and this made me feel a bit self-conscious. I was kind of relieved when he left. Jonas would usually go with Michael when he would go out with Megan. Ashley was never invited to go with her and that would make her upset. A lot of people fail to understand that siblings are affected by the condition that their siblings have. Everything was always being altered, and schedules being changed due to Michael's needs were always hard for her to understand. So, she felt ignored and pushed aside. So, it was hard for Ashley to cope with being Michael's sister. She was always in the shadow of Michael, to where she was hidden away. This in fact made her feel like she was being treated differently because she was the healthy one. This I know sounds crazy. So, when a child is terminally ill in the house, it affects everyone, and the family dynamic is altered.

For Halloween Peter picked up Ashley, Jonas, and me to go trick-or-treating over where Megan lives. Michael was already at their house. There were a lot of houses over there, and it was a much safer area. On the way, Peter had a talk with me about my living situation. He made it clear that Nessa and Junior were using me. I already knew that, and I wanted Nessa and her kids out. Junior already had a place with his new girlfriend and cousin. I found some letters around the house that were left on purpose. The letters stated how she was sick of living in Chicago. The letters were to various people in Florida, possibly other friends she never mentioned. The real thing going on was the fact that Nessa did not like that her ex was with someone else. It is kind of like; she did not want him until someone else did. She claimed illness tonight, so she did not have to be a mother to take Jonas out for Halloween. We pulled into a house that was really big and beautiful, just like Michael said. We all went in and sat down in the living room, which was huge. I met his wife, Gale, who was on the tall side, blond hair and skinny. She was like a happy go lucky pop tart. She had so much energy. I met all the other kids as well. There was Alan who was aa couple years younger than his older sister Megan. He was very tall, with blond hair and on the thin side. Then there were the twins Molly and Marlon, both had brown hair, average height, and size for their age. So, we all went trick-or-treating and had a lot of fun. Afterwards, we came back to the house and had pizza. While we were eating, I had to play twenty questions with Megan's parents. They certainly had a lot of questions concerning my family. Around 9pm the kids started to get tired, so Gale drove us home.

    On the way home she asked more questions about things going on in my life. So, I just told her a few things and she started to overreact like it was too much for her ears. How do these people function? I guess, living in their perfect world with no real problems other than trying to analyze people like us, fills their day. On the other hand, holding fundraiser events makes them feel good and like they did something to help people who are regular people. The truth is, there are more of us than them. After this ride, I really wanted to distance myself from their family, but they had other plans. Once inside the apartment, I saw Nessa seemed to have recovered from her so-called illness. I was glad to be back in my comfort zone and I am sure Gale felt the same.

## CHAPTER TWELVE

# BLIND EYES

Things started to go more downhill with Nessa and her kids being there. The main reason was because of the war Nessa was creating with the kid's father. It was over between the two of them, but Nessa was trying to break-up Junior and his new girl. She would disappear at night when she did not have class and go to his house to cause trouble. She talked about slitting his tires and stuff like that. I also found out she was smoking weed in a car out front. Junior would join her and a few others. This was before he moved out. But then I heard she was not going to class somedays and Junior was picking her up and they would hang out. So much for the girlfriend at home. It was getting to be too much for me.

Then I had to cope with Michael's ever-changing condition. Every visit to the doctor was always unwelcome news, which is why I started referring to the doctors at the MDA as the "bad news doctors." They were always so negative. They would say, "Well, he's getting weaker." That is difficult to hear as a mother. Just too many doctors for Michael's care. He had of course, his pediatrician, pulmonologist, cardiologist, physical therapist, three orthopedics, brace specialist, nutritionist, and two neurologists. Then there was the care coordinator and the wheelchair guy (as Michael called him).

I really needed some support from Nessa, but she was not much of a friend to me anymore. I felt so alone. So, after the kids went to bed, I called Magic. I could always count on him for more than enough support. He also sent me several letters that I have not responded to, as of yet. I know, I am so bad when it comes to writing back. I am just so overloaded with all this stuff. But he is so sweet, patient, and understanding. So, I just needed to vent. I know what he is going to say, "Cut them loose and have you given any thought to moving here with me?" I know he is right about cutting them loose, but how? Maybe she will go back to Florida. I hope soon.

As far as moving with Magic is concerned, I really don't think that is a promising idea. We are friends, but I know it would be a great escape. I do not want to rely on him or anyone else. People pull you in with their generosity, and then then once they get you hooked—then you're stuck. They start to control you, your decisions, and visions. I wanted to accomplish things and reach my full potential on my own. I also had some trust issues and letting people in was hard. People have alternative motives. People seem to always want something in return. What did Megan's family want in return for their kindness? I did not really know these people, and I also did not realize things when they were happening. This was a mistake on my part. Later on, Michael would mention some comments which were beliefs the family had about people like us.

I had a lot to deal with and just wanted to find peace in my life. I was still healing from the scarring. I had the greatest kids in the world. Michael never complained about anything. He was such a trooper when it came to dealing with all this MD stuff. He was just like any other kid, really. He loved to play video games, draw, play on the computer, and he did not like schoolwork. Sounds typical, right? But this thing he has, was silent, but I worried constantly about him. I tried to block all my fears out of my mind so it would not show. When terminal entered my mind, I tried to block it with happy thoughts. I was feeling submerged by water, like I was drowning or choking. The feelings came back, perhaps some unresolved issues from when I was in foster care and my world was out of control; all I wanted to do was fly away. I used to have water dreams when I was a child and the only way to get to safety was to go across this bridge which was also surrounded by water. Slowly, I would start crawling across the bridge and then I would wake up. Come to think of it, I never did make it across the bridge, maybe that is why these dreams have returned.

I wanted the kids to have happy memories about their childhood, but not this condition that Michael had. I did not want my daughter to be traumatized by her brother's condition, but that was a challenging thing to do, even for the best of parents. Nobody really knew what Michael had or that it was terminal. I just called it the condition, but some people were nosier about why he was in a wheelchair. I just tried to ignore them. But sometimes that got hard when some people pushed it right in front of my face. Like on the bus one day, two women were trying to figure out why he was in wheelchair. Doesn't anyone mind their own business these days? Obviously, these women did not. They started implying, I was on drugs during my pregnancy. Really, people? I have never touched drugs, alcohol, and I do not smoke. I am definitely someone you never want to go for happy hour with. I am the most boring plain person alive and none of that interests me.

A week before Thanksgiving, I found out Nessa had lied to me about receiving her check. She told me she never got it, so she could not pay the current light or gas bill. While she was in the shower, she left her planner open face up and the check stub was right on top. Perhaps she planned it that way. When she got out of the shower, I confronted her. She admitted that she got it a week ago, but she did not pay the bills like she was supposed to. She claimed she did not think it was fair that she had to use her little check to pay bills. I was like OMG!! She does not pay for anything else. I used all my money on rent, cable bill, food, household supplies, personal items, and pay for all the laundry.

I had enough. I told her that she needs to move out as soon as she finds another place to go or go back to Florida. She said fine and called Junior to tell him that I was kicking her out right now. It was 11pm and the kids were asleep, so that is not what I was saying. But she wanted to leave and go live at Juniors, all because she wanted to start trouble. She started to pack her stuff along with the kids. Then she got them up and rushed them to the car when Junior arrived. Junior looked at me as he walked in and asked, "What was going on?" I shrugged and put my hands out, "I didn't say she had to leave now," I said. He figured as much, and he was no fool to what she was doing. But within 30 minutes they were all gone, and the house was quiet. I could not believe that this was all that was needed, so that she would leave.

The next day, she came by to pick up the rest of her stuff. Junior came in with some prescriptions from the doctor. Ashley and Kate had an appointment today with the same doctor. I called and canceled the appointment. I was so stressed and worried that Nessa would start some mess, depending on how her mood was. But when she arrived, she looked calm, but Junior looked totally stressed. I guess he would be after all, he had his new girlfriend and his baby mama living in the same house. I found out that the light and gas bill had not been paid for almost 3 months. So, I had to use the money that Magic sent me to pay it. I was so annoyed with the situation that I will never let anyone else ever live with me unless we take marriage vows!

My friend Manny would get Michael off the bus, now. Ashley went to daycare until 6pm and then I would pick her up before coming home. I went to school three days a week and worked the other four days. So, I was busy, but I noticed once they moved out that the kids were calmer and more behaved. Sometimes tension causes kids to react. Now, the tension was gone and so were the issues. We celebrated Thanksgiving with Manny and the kids. It was a quiet day followed by the weekend. The holidays came so fast, and I was not prepared. But Megan's family bought Michael an X-box which was nice. I just bought them some new clothes and a few toys. They were always happy and appreciative. I am so lucky to have kids like I do.

## CHAPTER THIRTEEN

# People Looking In

In March there was a fundraiser for Michael. It was through a foundation of Gale and Peter, called Happy Foundation. I was told a few weeks before the event, so that I could prepare myself. I was not so sure I wanted to be the beneficiary of such an event, but I was not asked for my opinion. I was only told when and where to be. Michael did not understand what this all meant but started asking questions. I was incredibly nervous and had never attended anything like this. Manny came along with us. It was a wonderful thing they did for us, but I really wanted to talk with the children first and then make a decision if this was a good thing for our family. They only asked Michael. This occurrence of only asking Michael and treating him like an adult to make decisions would eventually take a toll by adding unneeded stress. This would also lead to them making decisions with Michael, like they are the parents.

    I tried to go with the flow during the event because I did not like to be the center of attention or attraction. I surely did not like to be a spectacle with strangers parading around me. After some videos played of boys with Muscular Dystrophy made Michael really sad, he wanted to leave. The pictures were disturbing, and we were seeing his journey with this condition before it happened. I do not think they initially wanted to cause hurt feelings with the videos and pictures. They did raise a lot of money for the MDA and the other amount was to buy a house for our family. On a positive note, I was shocked and surprised about the house, but little disturbed by the images on the videos showing a very skinny young boy being carried and put into the bed. He looked very weak, and it me think about Michale's future. At that moment, my joy and excitement for what the family was trying to achieve with us was overshadowed with the reality of what condition he had and his future without a cure.

A newspaper article came out a week later with Megan and Michael on the front cover. After reading the article I saw something that really started to bother me. The question of what the family wanted was starting to waver to me. As a mother of a child who probably wouldn't even reach the age of eighteen, that we were being used. By that way I mean, not financially--but to put it out there that we were the poor unfortunate family. The article made Megan and her family come out as the heroes. They were saving the poor family. The article stated that I was "blunt in telling Michael about his disease." Blunt? Really? I was being as honest as I could be--in the most elementary and sensitive way. Michael knew too much already from when he went to camp. They had no idea what I was going through. Let them walk in my shoes for a bit.

Honestly, I did not want to know all the horrible things that my son was going to experience, but I was not sheltered from that because I am his mother. It is always nice to be the family that just looks in our life like they are looking through a glass, while they apply a band-aid whenever they choose to fix something their way. Michael needs more than a band-aid and someday they might actually see beyond what they see now. Then there was the speech at the fundraiser, Peter said that we lived in the inner-city. Really? Have they ever seen the inner city? We did not live in the inner city. Why is it that every time a family from upper class sees another family living somewhere in Chicago, they assume that it is always the inner-city. It is always, "those people" and "people like that," used to describe us. The word ghetto even surfaced into the conversation to make the story more significant. The rags to riches story always makes a room full of suits with a cause feel better about themselves. Maybe, just another reason to give themselves a pat on the back to illustrate, a job well done. I feel like they put us in a box with a label.

Several people kept their eyes on me the entire night. It made me feel self-conscious and out of place. This entire fund raiser was beyond me. I needed to have an adequate class for this kind of event. I really did not know how to deal with all this attention. I was a simple person who has never been given anything unless I have earned it myself. In my life, if you took something, there was always a price to pay--one way or another. Now these people were donating money and interested in helping my son and our family. I never wanted to owe anyone anything, but now I was in a situation where nothing was what I am accustomed to.

I was approached by a few men in suits and woman dressed very classy. They looked me up and down, and gave praise to our family, while giving total gratitude to the family who put this together. They laid pity on our family and said how it makes them feel so good to give to the less fortunate. I was given a few envelopes with money and checks for amounts I have never seen in my life. I tried to refuse each one of them after looking inside, but each one of them would put their hand up, refusing to take it back. They all had the same reasoning to why they gave the money to me versus giving it to the foundation. One woman even said, "Shush," while putting her finger over her mouth. So, all of this was highly unusual, unconventional, yet remarkably interesting. I guess, I was a bit of all three, but being unconventional was one of the most interesting things about me. The night was over, and we were free to go after playing polite recipients for the moment. We did not get too far because our car broke down and they gave us a ride home. I felt a bit embarrassed by this, as Manny stayed with the car. I guess this moment would change our lives more than I know, as we arrived home late and tired. Michael had an interesting night, as he would say to me at bedtime. I totally had the same feeling, more than he knew.

Like I said earlier, a portion of the money raised was to be used for a new house for our family with wheelchair accessibility. The house was to be located in the North-Suburbs, not too far from my college and where there is transportation. That is why I was shocked when I was told the new location of the house. I did not want to sound unappreciative, but they were making decisions for my family without understanding the complete picture. Remember, what I said about the family looking through a glass? Well, this was one of those moments. This was also one of those moments in which I saw, we know, and you don't. There would be many of these moments during this arrangement and perhaps friendship? The house that was supposed to be in the North-Suburbs ended up taking us to Palatine, which was an hour from Chicago. So, even know the location was not where I wanted it, I still went to see our new place that was chosen. It was a condominium versus a house, but it was still great. It was a quiet area full of potential. The school was just down the street. It was so different from Chicago. For instance, it was so quiet with not too many cars or people. Harper College was not too far away. Gale said that there was transportation just down the street from the house. I stopped by the kids' school to get some information. We really were not here just seeing the place--we were here to agree to move. Gale said that she could not find anything else, so this would be a good place. Afterwards, we went to lunch at Wendy's and headed back to Chicago.

I was not so sure if I wanted to move from where I was living in Chicago. It was not so bad, not really and I have seen worse. I was really scared, and this was taking me out of my comfort zone. There was a lot of pressure to move to Palatine because this was the best option, but I was not so sure. A week later, I was being rushed by Gale who purchased the property in Palatine and became a section 8 landlord just so I could use the voucher to stay in the program. Deciding to request the moving papers to get the process going was a hard decision to make. I drove out to Palatine with Manny, so that he could see the area. We went to the condominium, the college and looked around for the so-called transportation. What had we found out was disappointing? The college was too far to walk to and there was no real transportation like Chicago and the Metra did not go to the college. There was one bus that went to the school, however, you had to walk ten blocks to get to it. Then it only ran a few times a day and you had to flag it down—which was different. Manny was not moving here with us, so I had no car, and no license.

So, after we drove back home, I called Gale to tell her I could not move there because of the transportation. She got upset and said that I would have to figure it out. I felt like I did not have a choice and I was expected to move. I protested because I had a bad feeling about it. But even Peter said that we had to move because they had already made a mortgage payment on the property. I really did not have a choice either because my Section 8 was already transferred, so we would have to wait for the inspection. This was the next step in the process and would be the only thing that would prevent us from moving there.

A week later the inspection took place and passed with only the toilet needing to be replaced in the hallway bathroom. After hearing the news of the inspection, I made plans for the move. This was a big move from the city of Chicago to the Suburbs. I went to the college to pick up my transcripts which turned out to be very awkward. I got on the bus and there was Nessa. She looked up and motioned for me to sit with her. I was a bit shocked to see her because I thought she went back to Miami. She was at the college for the same reason as me (picking up transcripts) and after she headed back to Miami with the kids. I told her my news about moving, and she was excited that we were going to the suburbs. We went into the school together but would get off at different stops on the way home. I knew this was goodbye.

Junior was much happier, and he told me that Nessa was a bit jealous and wished she were coming too. Our visions and dreams were different, which put us on different paths. The truth is, she and I were like day and night. We had next to nothing in common, but were brought together in passing, while running away from challenges. I never saw Junior, Nessa, or the kids again. They (Nessa and the kids) left for Miami and Junior left the Country to Honduras. I accepted my move to Palatine as changes can be good. I packed up and rented a U-Haul. We moved on May 27, 2005, from Chicago to Palatine.

Gale and Peter kept the kids while we loaded up and made the move. They meant well, they really did. But sometimes comments would be said that were out of place. I knew from where they stood, it sounded right to them. But some of the comments sounded more like they were talking down to me and at me, instead of to me. I had a positive aspiration about moving there, but I was worried. I decided to keep it to myself because they did not get it. How could they possibly understand what I was feeling? I tried asserting myself when telling her that that moving here was going to be difficult due to the transportation issue, but I was shut down. I never tried again. Later that night, they dropped off the kids. The children were happy here, but it was not Chicago. One thing that was different was the race of people around here was mainly white. There was an area on the other side of Palatine that had Hispanic people. But Michael and Ashley were categorized as Black. They had some other racial mixture in them which made Michael look more Hispanic, but not Ashley. Funny how the same genes fall. There were only a handful of Black kids. We were not prepared for such prejudiced views.

## CHAPTER FOURTEEN

# THE BURBS AND UNWELCOMING VOICES

It was Memorial weekend when we moved in, so we had the entire weekend to get everything in order. I made two beds on the floor for the kids. Then I made a bed on the floor for myself in the bedroom. The first night in our new house was the hardest. It was so quiet that I could not sleep, so I went to look out the window. There were a few stores across the street and a pizza place. A bit later, I tried to lay down and try this sleeping thing again. I turned on the television, so I could hear something to help make me fall asleep. The next day, the furniture was delivered. The kids and I got new beds. There was also a new couch and love seat. All of this was purchased with the funds from the fundraiser. I was very appreciative of what the family had done for us. Nobody had ever done anything like that for me. I had never allowed anyone to help because I had some trust issues, but I gave their family trust.

I worked hard over the weekend to get everything put up--and to make the place look great. Magic called as he did every day. He had already written me three letters that were in the mailbox when I moved in. The next day, I got four more letters. He was overseas right now and was busy, as usual. Soon he wanted me to take the kids to California and he was planning to be back at the end of July. We both had busy lives. But talking on the phone is great. I did not feel so alone when we talked. He was alone too, yet troubled. I needed someone to be there for me, but I was always expected to know the answers and solve everyone else's troubles.

I always looked as the "strong one." Sometimes that label becomes hard to live up to with way too many expectations. I was always complimented by people in my life of how I have perspectives that help them. I do try, but I am still trying to figure me out.

The kids start school on Tuesday, and they were excited. Michael took the bus and Ashley I had to walk to school. Since Michael was in a wheelchair he qualified for bussing. However, since we only lived 2 blocks away, Ashley did not qualify for the bus. I had a meeting on the first day of school for Michael. We all sat around a big, long brown table in the conference room. I noticed there were a lot of smiles which were very welcoming. I had my guard up due to the experiences I had in Chicago. But, to my great surprise and hope--everything went great. Michael was given an assistant to be with him all day. And he was put in regular education and there was no fighting. Michael got the best of the best. He deserved that and more.

After this meeting I let my guard down, but this could have been my first mistake when dealing with the school with its very white surroundings. There was a race and color issue in Palatine that was hidden away. The message was--all was not welcome. So, while everything fell into place with Michael, Ashley on the other hand would face the harshest, critical, and racist display of discrimination and bullying. It started from the first day she started school.

Ashley was excited and nervous to start a new school as most children are. I was happy that they would be at the same school. From the start there were stares from others. Either from racial predjustice, ignorance, stereotypes, and special needs discrimination. The questions came months after the stares started. The questions were like no other, but any parent or child who is mixed has been challenged with such things, and the stories that people would generalize through their gossiping groups were just like, really?

After the first day of school, Ashely ran to her room. Shortly after, I heard things being thrown and the closet. I walked into her room and noticed all her dolls, toys on the shelves and around the room were gone. After looking closer, I noticed only the dolls of any ethnicity and color other than white were gone. As a parent, you then start to think, "Did something happen today? Did I miss something?" Ashley went to school that day excited, but things did not go well for her. She was questioned about her color and why she looked the way she did. There were no other children of color in her room. Several of the students wanted to know the reason she did not have skin like them and why she did not look like me (her mother). So, all day was question after question with no end. Questions like, "Where are you from?" "You don't look like your mom." "Are you adopted?" "Your skin color is different from your mother, why is that?" "Your hair looks so different." Ashley decided after all of these questions, which being just white was better. So, she threw all her Black and dolls of color in the closet. Came out of her room and said, "I have decided I just want to be white-no Black and no brown skin for me. I want to erase the brown color because it's different and ugly." The other girls have long blonde and brown hair that is so different from mine and beautiful." Wow, that was a lot. It was at that moment that I wished she came with a manual, especially at times like this. This moment will be what shapes her as a person as she grows up and discovers who she is. This moment could be when she realizes she has socialized into what others define beauty as. This moment could be a lot of things.

So, as I thought of what to say to her, many things went through my head. I knew at this current moment in time there would be more future moments like this one. I looked down at my light-skin and I knew I would never be able to tell her that I know what it's like to be disliked because of my race or color of my skin. I have not seen much of that in my life to be held as truth. A few moments of mean words do not constitute remotely what she is going through or will.

So, I explained what the kids said at school was wrong. She repeated, "They are wrong?" We had a conversation that she would never be just white or have skin like me. She would eventually have darker skin than she does now and features like her father would be more evident. She protested that she wanted my skin and my hair. She was frustrated with the fact that Michael had my hair. "Why does he have your hair mommy." she said. She felt she should have had my hair because she was the girl. This was an extremely hard moment for her. Living in a mainly all white area where children have made the rules; white is beautiful, and Black is not, has already started some bad feelings about this place. I was hoping that the kids would just accept her for who she was without all the comments of being different. I hoped over time they would see the similarities and her beauty. Throwing all her dolls of color in the closet would not change the fact of who she already was. But perhaps she felt not seeing them look back at her everyday was an escape from how they were making her feel. In time when she is ready, she may take the dolls out of the closet and sit them back on the shelf with the white dolls. All of her mixtures have blended her into the person she is already. Perhaps when she gets older, she will see that. All in suitable time. However, this incident would leave a scar from unwelcoming committee her school.

Ashley and Michael spent just a few weeks at Winston Campus, until school finished for the year. Then the kids started day camp at Salt Creek for the entire summer. Michael had an aide from NWSRA, named Kelly. She was truly short, thin with long blonde hair. I was concerned if she was going to be strong enough to pick him up, but she was actually stronger than she looked. She was exceedingly kind and sweet to Michael as well. He always had fun no matter where he was or the situation. He was always strong-willed and always made the best of everything he touched. Ashley on the other hand was different and often would struggle. Ashley met a friend at the camp named Yoshie. She was the same age, long dark hair, and she was from Japan. Her father was in Japan working on some project. The mother would drop her off at camp every morning. The two girls were remarkably close, shared lunches, and cultures. The girls would call each other on the weekend. Ashley seemed so happy with her new friend. As a mother, I was happy to see her make a friend to smile and laugh with. It was a turning point for the move and for Ashley. Summer camp was a positive event for both Michael and Ashley.

I attended college at Harper over the summer and worked at the Academic & Counseling Center in the I-building. The staff there was genuinely nice and appreciated the help. I would do typical work like answering phones, filing, making copies and checking-in students when they came to see a counselor. Michael went to the MDA camp once again. In early July, Megan, Michael, Ashley, and myself went to the Carnival. It was just a few blocks away, so we just walked. I paid for myself, and Megan paid for herself and the kids. Her parents were always generous with giving her money to spend on them. So, we went ride to ride and had a lot of fun.

Michael had his eye on the "Fun Room." I told him that he could not go into the room because he would have to be carried through it and something bad could happen. I thought we had an understanding, but obviously Megan did not agree with something. So, while I was on the Ferris wheel with Ashley, Megan decided to take Michael to the fun room against my wishes. She, after all, was just a kid herself. After I got off the ride with Ashley, I did not see Michael or Megan. So, I looked around and that is when I heard a scream. It is scary moment when a mother hears her child's scream.

Mothers tend to always know their child's calling. But what happened was serious. Megan was carrying Michael from the fun room. He was crying because his leg was hurt. Apparently, she took him down the slide, while she was sitting down with him, his leg went underneath her leg and she sat on it. She rushed us home and then just left. She said she had to go to work. Really? I had no car to take him to the doctor or hospital. She took no responsibility for what she did. I told her not to go into the fun room, but she does not listen. This was really the beginning of seeing that Megan does what she wants no matter what. Then instead of taking responsibility, she runs behind her parents to oversee the situation. She was not responsible as her parents wanted to think. The kids would come home and tell stories about some of the things she was doing. Megan could do whatever she wanted with no real consequences.

On Sunday, I took Michael to the hospital and his leg was broken. So, they said I had to take him to the Bone & Joint Institute. He then was put in a cast for 6 weeks, so I was not going to send him to the MDA camp this year. The doctor there said that this was serious, and I need to rethink the friendship between my son and Megan. The doctor called her irresponsible. When I called her mother to let her know that it was broken, she only said how sorry her daughter was. If she were so sorry, she would have taken him to the hospital, but she did not. So, I told her mom that Michael would not be going to the camp. Gale argued she had already arranged to borrow a van to take him to the camp. Then she went on and on about how Michael should be able to go to the camp in a cast. So, in the end I caved.

## CHAPTER FIFTEEN

# Brown Skin In White Suburbia

Ashley always would make friends with the one child of color that was around or the one child who was not white. She did this over the summer at camp when she met Yoshie. They remained friends until the end of camp and then she and her mother moved back to Japan. Every weekend she would call Ashley, sometimes waiting until Ashley was finished with dinner. I thought her parents gave their young daughter permission; however, her parents were shocked when their phone bill came. It revealed how much their daughter had been calling the States. There were times that Yoshie would wait until Ashley would take a bath before talking. Then there was the one time I noticed the phone was off the hook, and when I said hello, a little voice was there. Her father took the phone and was very polite while asking how we were doing. When Ashley came to the phone, she always had such an enjoyable time talking with her friend. She learned a bit of Japanese. This was her first best friend. Her parents noticed that when their daughter was in the States, that Ashley was the only friend of Yoshie. I guess they knew what it was like to be friendless, so they stuck together.

While Michael struggled with having a physical special need, Ashley would get tormented because of the color of her skin, and this led to bullying. Palatine seemed to have some hidden race issues. Michael maintained looking very Hispanic with light brown skin. Ashley, however, first started to change at three, when her curly brown hair and other features from her father appeared. These features would only get stronger in the coming years. Michael never suffered any harsh or racial discrimination. Ashley was not so lucky. In Chicago, Ashley was accepted, however there were a few instances of extra questions or stares from people. Here it was different. Ashely was taking gymnastics in the evenings over the summer and there were these two beautiful girls in Ashley's class. They were from Ethiopia but were adopted by white American parents.

One day, the mother of the girls asked what Ashley was mixed with? I told her Liberian. She gave me the look, and responded very much, like I know she then started with all these questions. I almost started to entertain her by answering them, but in the end, I stopped myself. She assumed Ashley and Michael were adopted. As much as I said, they were not adopted, she went on and on. I just nodded my head, while excusing myself, and getting out of there. Looking at Ashley, you can tell she is mixed with something. In this world, she is either white or nonwhite. The best of each world is sometimes hidden from people who choose what they see. Her feelings and the sense of belonging was already being challenged since moving here.

There was only a small percentage of Black kids at the school. And when I say small, I mean less than five. Ashley and a classmate named John, were the only two kids in grades 1-4. There were no Black teachers at the school, either. There were a few Hispanic teachers' that taught the bilingual rooms from K-4th grade. The social worker, Ms. Angel was also Hispanic, and was genuinely nice. Ashley soon found she was not welcomed here like the white kids. It all started with the discrimination that came from the stereotypes and prejudices that would later lead to passive aggressive racism. These things were always blamed on it being a misunderstanding. Was it really?

Remember the story from kindergarten with the dolls? She was learning messages from gymnastics and camp. Then there were the stares and the judgements that came and went. When kids attack the color of skin, it is a tough concept for a child to understand. She said that the kids hate her. So, in Ashley's case, her thinking is to choose one race over another. "I will be white," but unfortunately it does not work that way. She wanted to look Hispanic like her brother with lighter skin. Having light skin, she felt would help her blend in with the white kids around this area. Especially, living in "white suburbia." She envied her brother Michael because he looked lighter and had hair like mine. Ashley was being programmed with the notion that white hair is pretty and black hair is ugly. What she saw on television did not help, either—not too many people of color with long beautiful hair, as she would say. I would google pictures to prove to her otherwise. Then she would protest by saying she did not see them in person every day. She was right about that, and I could not change it. As a parent I felt powerless. But I tried to remain positive and prayed it would get better.

I would ask for advice from Magic, and he always had some knowledge. But this time when I told him what was going on, he just cried. He couldn't believe this was happening, and he almost fell off his chair when I told him that she came home asking for bleach cream. Then after he was calm, he was able to give some kind words of how-to best handle this for Angel (his nickname for Ashley). I just wanted my daughter to feel loved and safe in her new surroundings. This was rough for Ashley and challenging for the family.

So, what do you say, when your skin is light, and you yourself do not know what it is like to have brown skin? I talk with her every day, telling her how beautiful she is. All I want her to grow up to be proud of who she is. Unfortunately, she is reminded every day that she is Black--by all the other children. They made up that she was adopted, just by looking at me--her mother. Since we did not match--as the kids called it. Where are the parents in this? One day, a little girl from our building came up to me, "Where did you get her from?" I was totally shocked by this 8-year-old. I simply said, "I had her, she is my daughter." The little girl looked puzzled. "No, that can't be true, she has darker skin." I responded, "She has a great tan." I walked away after that holding my daughter's hand. When I looked back, she was still standing there looking confused. I wondered what she was being taught at home or being exposed to.

Why do most white people see color first and features last? I noticed that mostly white people and other people of color outside the African American race tend to do this. Many believe that she is adopted, or I am her foster parent, or the best one was that her parents are in jail. When do I say she is my daughter their mouth drops? Then they feel out of place, they say, "I got Black friends with kids like yours." Yeah, really? Why is it, that a white person feels the need to say that? Many co-workers and friends of color who see Ashley's picture, their reaction is quite different. The first thing they will say, "Oh, wow, your daughter looks just like you. She has your bright eyes, smile, and nose." They will even say how her siblings look like her. For some reason, they can see and not just look. Other people are blinded by the color.

As Ashley grew up, she would look in the mirror and notice she was changing. Her hair was more like her dad's, her skin was getting darker, and lips were fuller. All these changes would start plenty of conversations with questions. This was an ongoing quest to understand. No matter how hard I tried to deprogram her—she would go back to school where the grooming of the majority was taking place. The assimilation to be white was the priority. The good, the bad, and the ugly were being preached to her. The other kids had, "white privilege." Their race was not thrown in their faces every day. An example, when a student called her out in front of the class, and said, "Aren't you Black?" Several of the kids in the class started laughing. Soon after, they asked, "Do you know who your real parents are?" Ashley felt out of place, so she walked away."

The other kids began to whisper while not one student defended her, and the teacher said nothing. Let the situation be reversed, "What if my daughter or the other student said something to the white kids?" It would be a big drama scene at their school, Winston Campus. Should the kids have been corrected? Yes, they should have been redirected. In my experience, kids only do what they see, and get away with what others just turn a blind eye. This becomes an everlasting behavior that perpetuates future behaviors. The age children need to be redirected is when they are this age. Her classmates began to slowly make comments, which lead to her being discriminated against. It always just takes one kid, who starts to spread hate around, and soon others joined in.

In "white suburbia" white privilege just passes by as an entitlement without even thinking about it. is hard to teach to white children. They just do not get it. I remember learning about the study by Jane Elliot, called, "Blue Eyes--Brown Eyes." This was used to instruct white kids about discrimination. We really need that study to be done here. But, not as a study, but a diversity class that begins in kindergarten. We could not get away with doing a study like these days. Remember, kids only do what they are allowed to do. It is up to the adults to reteach our children.

No one was going to do that at this school. Parents took no responsibility for what their kids would do. When you call someone out on the race talk of something their child did or something that has to do with race, people take to being defensive. It is not always that someone is calling you a racist. It is more about bringing awareness that there is an issue going on concerning race. Also, if you see your child saying remarks, then you as a parent can reteach your child. Where does this thinking come from? It usually is something or someone close to the child. Most of this is the result of white children being segregated from other races. First, the government segregated us and now we do it to ourselves. Chicago is one just big mess of segregation. We got a little everything. Everyone gets a piece of the pie in Chicago. Little Mexico, Poland, Russia, Germany, and Africa, and it goes on and on. When I was just a kid, I remember I was living in foster homes where I was the only light skinned person around. The girls said, "We are Black-- forget all that African American crap. And you, are just light skinned--not white. White is like the wall over there, as she pointed in that direction; so, you are not white." Being a foster kid no matter what color you are--we all belong to a tight sisterhood and brotherhood.

The biggest issue was these kids were allowed to say things to Ashley and get away with it. It really did not matter what they said to her because they would never get into trouble for the comments, I really would like these kids to go to Chicago to say these same comments as they do to my daughter. Over here. they don't see the real issue with saying such comments.

Michael was well aware of what things were being said to his sister. He saw the kids and how they treated her and how she was just left out. No adults would ever hear what was being said. They would only hear what Ashley would say. The other kids always denied it, making Ashley seem like a liar. Everyone always assumed that she had some issues because her brother was terminally ill. This only allowed the issue to be ignored and to continue. Others suggested that Ashley was being "sensitive." Why is it when a person of color tries to assert themselves about something that is wrongfully being said about them, the reason is that they are being sensitive. No one ever says that about the white people. That is very curious and concerning. The school had a concerning racial issue going on. So, between Michael's health issues and Ashley's issues of not being accepted, I felt like I didn't get a break.

## CHAPTER SIXTEEN

# BRIGHTER SMILES

Gale picked us up and we drove to Michael's MDA camp. Ashley came along this year to drop him off. The camp was in the same place as last year. The only change this year was that Megan's brother Alan was volunteering for the camp. Megan got Michael again only because she requested it and I agreed. The camp didn't really want her to have my son again. The MDA thought that Michael should be with another counselor. They told me that when they were together, they were like two children and rules were not followed last year when they were together. I had no idea this occurred. Michael was such a humble sweet child with a great personality which made everyone just love him. However, Alan ended up with a camper who was quite the opposite. He was grouchy and all he did was complain. As I passed by the two of them, all I could do was smile and laugh a bit. Not everyone gets a Mike.

Meanwhile, I took Michael to the cabin. Megan started showing us all the snacks, drinks, and other activities that she brought to the camp. There was a lot of stuff and I hoped that she was going to share it with the other kids in the cabin. I guess it was not fair that the other campers did not have the same. Sometimes people can overdue things a bit. So, we said our goodbyes for the week and started our drive home.

When we came to pick up Michael, he was tired from the long week. Michael's cast was wet, dirty, and ruined. Megan's dad said that he would pay for the new cast, but that never happened. I know that she did not mean for the cast to get destroyed. I certainly did not want her dad to have to pay for one. Her family has already done enough things for our family. I am not used to getting help, but the doctor was going to be mad because she had already given me a lecture. So, after we got home, I tried to clean off the cast as best as possible. I unpacked his stuff and washed his clothes. Michael went to bed early that night. The next morning, I got a call from the camp director at MDA. They reported again that this year some rules were not followed. The snacks and other things Megan brought to the camp were an issue. Then the night before the kids arrived, she ordered pizza for her cabin. The camp was not happy with that. Then there was the issue that she did not follow some other rules that lead to Michael's cast getting wet. So, they were saying the same thing the doctor stated previously, that I needed to put some separation between the two of them. Michael understood that Megan was just a kid. Her parents were always saying how mature she was for her age. Mature in some areas, maybe? But being responsible and making the right decisions for a child in her care was a completely different thing. She is not a bad person; shows a great lack of judgement as someone her age tends to do. It is that thinking, nothing bad will ever happen to me. Michael is my son and sometimes I feel that she is trying to take over.

There was finally going to be some separation anyway, Megan was going off to college. I have had some issues with Megan's friendship with Michael. It went from positive to manipulation. Everything was according to her schedule and hers alone. She would just call and say I wanted to pick up Michael. If I said no or we were doing something, she would get upset and try to get me to rearrange things for her. When that did not work, she would have her parents give me a call. They would plead with me, using this as her only day to see Michael. So, I felt pushed into allowing this to go on since her family has done so much. They did this massive thing when raising the money to buy a condominium for us and would pay for camps for the children in the summer. I said, thank you over and over. But just like I said thank you, over and over; this Megan always getting her way became a repetitive thing over and over. I felt that this would never end, or she would be satisfied unless she always got what she wanted.

Then there were other things, like how she acted around us. She didn't mean it the way it came out, but it made me feel awful. She knew that I was struggling, and her family was not. We were from two different economic classes. I never expected anyone from her class to help me. I wanted to do it all on my own. I did not want any comments about how I made them help me by pushing Michael off on them. I already heard some comments from her and her younger brother. I just tried to be forgiving. How much more thankful can I be? I thought the reward of giving was the happiness it brought to others, not expecting all the praise. She would take all of us out to lunch or dinner. She would rush of course because she had to be back home. It was nice for her to do these things, but if I refused, she would get upset. That would cause issues. Her mother owned the condominium I lived in, paid partially by the section 8 program. I did not want any issues, so I just agreed to it.

She would say the silliest things. For instance, we would have leftovers from the restaurant. she would say, "Well at least you have the food for later, do you want mine too." It was like, no we do not, we were not that poor. I do think that maybe she did not know what to say. Perhaps Megan did not know any better or how it was making us feel. Things she would say would just make us feel bad and lower than what we really were. Yes, I did get some help from the State with insurance and food. Once I finished college, I would not need the help anymore. That is why these programs exist, for a temporary solution. I did not want help forever. Gale said the plan was to give me the condominium after college and I would take care of the payments. All of that sounded good in the future.

Things were rough at times, so I was always happy to talk to Magic. His letters that came almost five to six a week were always comforting. He gave me so much inspiration even though he said that I inspired him. It went both ways though; I was there for him in many ways. We both had tough times, so being there for one another was important to us. Magic would always call around 9pm every night to check in. We would talk on the weekends for about three hours after the kids went to sleep. Afterwards, I would do some homework. Finding my focus and keeping my eye on the prize kept me going.

Over the summer, I learned my way around Palatine and got used to the place better than I thought I would. Manny would come for a few days and sleep on the couch. Then he would go back to his house on the weekend. It was hard living in Palatine with no car when he was not there. It made me depend on him, which I did not like. The summer went by fast and before I knew it, it was time for school to start. So, I went to get new book bags, supplies, clothes, and shoes. They were both excited to start school.

## CHAPTER SIXTEEN

# LIVING IN THE SHADOWS OF MICHAEL

On the first day of school, the kids were up bright and early. I put Michael on the bus, while Ashley and I walked up to the school. Ashley met her teacher on meet-the-teacher day, the day before school would start. She did not have the same challenges that Michael had physically. But she did have mental component, like worrying if the kids were going to like her. Ashley had issues with making faithful friends and was always second guessing herself. On the other hand, Michael had no troubles in school academically, socially, or emotionally.

He was a friend magnet, and kids were just naturally drawn to him. Being a mere genius always intrigued the other kids, but their curiosity about why he was in a wheelchair was always present. They were respectful into not asking. Ashley and Michael were treated differently by the kids at the school. The sad reality is that the school had some issues they did not want to talk about. There was a race stigma at the school, and it was unfolding in front of my eyes. While I got to see it through my daughter's eyes and through children/parent questions. Ashley had to live it each and every day. When you cannot be put into a box, there are always questions like, where are you from? Why is your hair different from ours? Wow, you are so exotic? Were you adopted? The questions seemed to never go away. So, for every question her brother was not asked, his sister was asked twenty. It never went away.

## MICHAEL: REFLECTIONS OF LIFE, LOVE, AND THE JOURNEY IN BETWEEN

Michael had an aide this year to help him in class and around the school. Her name was Ms. Carry, she was short, stocky, and had short brown hair. She just loved her job, and she loved Michael, of course. He also had an Individual Educational Plan (IEP) like all kids with a physical or mental special need. He did receive all sorts of accommodations which did help him have successes in school, while not self-handicapping him for the future. Michael attended regular ed while always being in the highest level for Math and Science. He loved being the smart kid in the classroom which gave him great self-confidence. Because he was so friendly and intelligent, most of the kids treated him just like anyone else. The kids did not see him as just a wheelchair or a disability. Once in a while a kid would say something negative and rude to him. He would come home from time to time telling me what they had said. Michael's overall experience in school was incredibly positive with the only exception of his occasional health interruptions.

The kids were well adjusted despite the challenges in the house. Ashley did not feel the difference in our family composition, and she did not see us as "special." At an early age, Ashley just knew of Michael and Mommy. She did not ask about her father. Then there was Manny who was just there. They never asked me if he was, "the boyfriend." At this point he was a friend. Ashley never asked about her brother's condition. She never asked why he could not walk and was in a wheelchair. Ashley asked nothing and just went with the flow. At times, I felt bad as a parent because so much of the focus was on Michael; with all his issues and all the doctor's visits, but she never complained. Michael never complained about being in a wheelchair or having this awful disease. The condition, as I referred to it--was kind of silent during this point in his life. He went to the MDA every six months only to hear the words, "he's getting weaker." Yeah, like I wanted to hear that. It causes great psychological and mental re-processing to inspire yourself with positive images as a parent, after visits to the MDA. Ashley watched on while observing all this talk, but she never knew Michael's true prognosis. In her mind, Michael was going to live forever. That is the way I wanted her to think. Knowing what is ahead becomes the torment that eats at your heart and becomes the curse.

Sometimes, ignorance is bliss. At times, it was difficult to manage things with being a mother, college student and working. As much as I tried to make myself feel like I belonged here in Palatine, I felt like I did not. I was a single mother, with little money, but I was living in an area where most of the residents made over $80,000 a year. In addition, they all had cars and so much more. The kids would come home asking, "When do we get to go on vacation? When do we get the house and the car?" Very natural questions for children to ask? I think so. But we did not blend too well within our surroundings. Little did I know, these feelings were not only shared by myself. Ashley felt that feeling not only because of how much money I did not make, but because of the color of her skin.

Everything was different over here. Halloween the kids got to get dressed up after lunch, and then have a party. The Trick-o-treating was from 3pm-7pm. So of course, I would rush home to take pictures before they went out. I was so proud of my children. They meant the world to me. For Thanksgiving, the kids had been out an entire week. I would make their incredibly special dinner with a turkey and all the trimmings. Michael loved pumpkin pie and spending time with his family, of course. Then for Christmas, we set the tree a few weeks before and decorated the entire house. Then we would open gifts on the day of. They had stockings filled with special snacks. This was only made possible by budgeting money throughout the year and only allowing one gift on their birthday and the rest for Christmas gifts. Megan's family would also bring some gifts for the family. I really didn't want anything. It was more important for the children. This was their day. Megan's family usually would bring their gifts a week before because they celebrated Hanukkah and would be on vacation during Christmas. This year, Megan brought the gifts over after getting home from college in Colorado. I didn't like it because I didn't have much of anything to give back. Due to the move this year, money was a little tight for anything else.

The kids were happy. It didn't take much to make the kids feel this way. They weren't greedy or anything like that, or didn't ask for anything. I had great children. They never complained about anything and were very loving. I was proud of them. They had a nice winter break and were ready to go back. School kept them busy and enjoyed going every day.

The year 2006 started out kind of challenging because Manny had a car crash and totaled his car. Gale got a donation to the foundation, and she used the money to purchase a used red wheelchair accessible red van for Michael. The van was shiny red and looked so beautiful. Michael loved the color red. Gale dropped it off in February just before his doctor's appointment in Chicago. Gale took some pictures before leaving. I was at school and Manny picked me up. It was so nice and very appreciated. I thanked Gale for the van because it was such a help to Michael, especially when you live in the burbs with no real transportation.

I did not like to put all my eggs in one basket when it came to anything--little, long a van I just received. I have known too many people who have had cars that looked good on the outside but kept breaking down and became unreliable quickly. What can I say? I have some trust issues and have learned to only have faith in myself. I have been disappointed and let down too many times as a child and an adult. I have been trained in the foster care system to expect the worst but hope for the best. It helps you prepare for things when things do go wrong.

This brings you to what happened next. So, in the morning the van wouldn't start, and I had to be in school. I was not too upset because of my mindset. I was more concerned that Mike had an appointment in Chicago. I could just take a cab or walk if I had to. Nothing stops me. I called Gale to let her know what was going on. She called the car place and they sent someone over to fix the issue. There was a piece that just blew, and they stated the reason was because the van was on the lot for so long. Michael went to his appointment and after that I went to school.

Of course, I got the same unwelcome news from the doctors. In addition, Michael needed a tendon release procedure done. So, I made an appointment during Spring break. Other than that, it was the same-old-same-old. Michael was getting weaker, which was much of the lingo of this terrible disease. On the minor side, he needed some new braces, but the orthopedic didn't want to see him until after the surgery to make the braces. He also started to see a pulmonologist and cardiologist at Lutheran General Hospital. This was the beginning of Michael seeing every kind of doctor that was out there--just about.

It was hard to leave an appointment always hearing such negative but very real things about my son. I then had to sit in class with all this on my mind. The words from the doctors just replayed in my mind over and over. I would always put a smile on my face, masking how I really was feeling. It was the only way to get through these tough times. Sometimes, while I was daydreaming of Michael as a toddler running through the house trying to wear my shoes. His smile lit up the room, and I could just picture him trying to walk in those big shoes that just made me laugh. Sometimes, one of my classmates or Professors would ask, "Is everything, ok?" I would just smile and say, "Everything is great." It was just easier to say that because people don't really want to know too much and defiantly do not want the conversation to get too emotional. I have had a couple of people get very demanding to know about Michael and what it is like to have a child who is terminal. You take a deep breath, and you start to say a bit more than the others. Then you see their faces, and you stop. Michael's condition was a very scary thing while terminal word gives you chills down your back, and death of a child just leaves you frozen.

When you have other children, as I did in the house, you have to make sure the other child is not stuck. Sometimes, the other child just gets lost in the terminal illness of their sibling and becomes the brother's keeper. I had to find balance in the craziness of Michael's illness. That is hard at times and trust me when I say that even in the best of circumstances of any parent that goal is often not met. Parenting often has challenges, but this thing that Michael was battling for was horrific. But it was the family's battle as well. I always try to push his prognosis out of my mind, but sometimes it would push its way through. Those days were tough.

Ashley found an outlet through her talent for gymnastics. Ashley started at Rolling Meadows Club. She had some real talent and was impressive strong for her age. So, she went two times a week. I wasn't sure, if I wanted her in gymnastics because I was worried about injuries and all. I already spent so much time at the doctor with Michael that I didn't need injuries. But she needed a distraction from all this stuff going on with her brother, so I allowed it. Gale used the money from the foundation to pay for her gymnastics, other activities, camps during the winter break and summer vacation. This was a major help with the childcare for them. Sometimes, they had days out of school, and I didn't. The kids were lucky.

For some reason, Megan had it in her head that the kids would be deprived if they did not get to do these things like she did. They were not deprived at all. I did feel at times that they felt sorry for them. We did not want pity, and we expected nothing from anyone. We were not alone in having a child diagnosed with a terminal illness; like the one Mike had, nor for the many children who have the same thing or something else. Gale sometimes looked confused about what to do. Sometimes, I just needed to vent, but they would try to reach in and fix the problems as quickly as possible. Looking from the outside it must seem that's all that was needed was money, but that was wrong.

Sometimes the abled people don't try to understand the issues, so they keep putting a band-aid on the wound. Sometimes, looking deeper at the issue can help with making a more subjective call on things. Every time there was an issue, they would use the band-aid theory, which caused more issues to arise. They were looking through a looking glass and they would look at us as incapable or special. This blinded them from really seeing us. They just knew the issue-not the person who underneath. Many people do this to other people not aware of how that makes them feel. It does not make them bad people because at least they tried to tap into the world of someone that they would not have ordinarily even known.

Our paths crossed, but I honestly believe we impacted their lives, as lessons learned in life. These lessons are not taught in school and there is no degree high enough to begin to understand. But on the other hand, there was a connection with high impact. This connection will be remembered on our part forever. I will remember them, but will they remember Michael and us? Through the pain, comes letting go, and accepting what will happen. After it is all over, sometimes forgetting is just a way to end the pain and move on. Everyone has their way. Only time will tell how Megan's family will react. Being there when things are not so bad is one thing, but truly is another to be there at the end.

## CHAPTER SEVENTEEN

# A Million Miles Apart

Megan had issues dealing with things about Michael. She would ask questions about things she should not ask. There were boundaries often crossed by her and the family. So, after his surgery, she challenged why he needed the surgery if he was in a wheelchair? He had to have the tendon release because his toes were pointing down like a ballet dancer, and shoes could be an issue. Since we live in a cold state, he needs something on his feet. Then she asked the question if Michael was going to be on a ventilator? As of now, I told her no. Michael wished not to be on one, so I would honor that. I guess, that was not good enough for her so, she did what she usually did when she did not hear something she liked. She called her mother to complain. So, her mother calls me and says, "You should not have conversations with my daughter about our vent decisions." She felt that I would make the right decision and put him on the ventilator when the time came. Really? No, if Michael said no--it would be no. So, it is amazing when Megan does something inappropriate or says something wrong to our family, it is totally ok. But she does not play by the same rules, how interesting. These things that Megan would do, which I would refer to as trying to play rank; this just made me feel bad and created a wedge between our family and theirs.

So, dealing with all this stress was difficult. Megan created stress I did not need. I did not hear too much from dad or from Molly. But when I did, there were always comments and twenty questions.

Then I had the stresses from Michael having this annoying thing and all the issues with that. Then there was Ashley being the sister of the child with the condition, was hard.

She didn't get the attention she deserved and was treated differently by their family. The foundation paid for her gymnastics, but often she was treated as the sidekick. She felt unimportant and brushed aside. Then there were the stresses from being in school and working. I was trying to keep all A's so that I could get the scholarship for the four-year university. So, I had to work twice as hard.

In the Spring, Michael had the surgery at Rush Hospital in Chicago. We had to be there at six in the morning. Michael was so brave, and it did not seem to faze him. It was just another medical procedure on his growing list that just came along with the disease. He never complained about them. I would always talk to him in a positive manner that we're in this together and always there to take care of him. Making these moments pleasant and pushing through them for the sake of the children was all I could do. For the most part, as hard as it was, I succeeded. The surgery was about one hour and then he was back in recovery. By one o'clock in the afternoon, we were home. The recovery was less than what the doctor said. Michael was ready to go back to school when break was over. He somehow always healed faster than what the doctor would say. That is a blessing and there was someone looking over him, beyond our reach.

It was during this time; Michael spoke of two men who came to visit him in his room at night. The light was shut off every night, but in the morning, it was on. There was no explanation for this. But then Michael started talking about these two men and maybe, they left the light on. He had a whole mouth full to say about these two beings and the dreams he had with them in it. Was it real? Or was he dreaming? What was really curious was the fact he described them as messengers. One of them was peaceful with positive vibes- giving him peace and joy. The other one was a bit quiet with few words and used more gestures. He said to Mike, according to his words, "Do not fear—you are not alone. You will find love and peace." He then asked me, "What is a guardian angel?" "Why do they say, I will always be close to my sister and mommy?" Wow, this appeared to be an act of faith. Our faith had been shaken since he was diagnosed.

My faith was always strong in my young years as a child in foster care. I would talk to God as he was my only faithful friend. I was able to find peace, hope, and strength through my conversations with this being. He was being touched by someone incredibly special. Perhaps, they were preparing him for something bigger. I do not think Mike was making this up. I would feel the presence of something in his room. There was a feeling of peace, love, harmony, which just gave me this warm feeling in my heart. Just like when I was a child, it gave me courage and the strength to survive. I needed that for strength. These two beings I never saw, but only felt them. They remained part of Michael's world and they never left him until the time was right.

Over the summer, I just worked at the school which gave me a break. Michael and Ashley went to the camp once again. Michael went to the MDA camp in June. He had a different counselor this year and had a lot of fun. We spent the rest of the summer going swimming in the back of the condominium. We even went to Megan's house to swim. It was nice going over there to enjoy the pool, but it was tainted a bit. Then there were all the questions being asked. It was always the same questions. They were highly creative in the way they would present the questions. They were trying to figure me out, along with Manny. They would not ask questions straight out, which was annoying.

I didn't like taking anything from them. Some people can feel taken by people, so I didn't want them to feel that way. I wanted to do everything for my own family. But it was during this time that some comments were made when Michael was around at their house. There were certain questions being asked that were inappropriate. Mainly, the questions were coming from Megan and Marlon. They would ask questions about my job, me being in school, and make statements about not wanting to come around when I was home. Michael got the opinion they did not like me very much and wanted to keep their distance. Michael said that Peter thought I was odd and strange. He felt that I was immature and didn't think I knew what I was doing. Peter thought I was stuck in the situation I was in because of the bad decisions I was making. So, did he have all the answers?

I think not. One of the many decisions included letting Nessa and Junior live with me. But on a positive note, he said that I was a good person, highly intelligent, positive, and motivated to make things better. Michael did not know what to think of these conversations, other than they made him feel uncomfortable. Michael made it clear that if it were not for him, they would not be around at all. Well, I already knew that. That's what brought us together in the first place, Megan meeting Michael.

In early August, Megan went back to college and Alan started college as well. Then Michael, Ashley and I started school, so we were busy. I had five classes this semester which kept me so busy and unavailable to unnecessary drama. I had to stay focused and motivated to achieve my educational goals. I also had to have a straight head on my shoulders and maintain my mental health. With all the stress filled with unfortunate events in my life and the children's life, I had to have a positive outlet. My outlet was writing, meditation, and listening to motivational classical music. I had to keep peace as my center and learn to shut out the drama that sometime can invade that peace. This is survival 101 when having a child with special needs and terminal illness with emotional support.

Time management was key here and thank God, I was blessed with strength, and personality type A! There were moments of doubt, sadness, and disappointment of why me? But then I would snap out of that kind of thinking and say aloud that we are not the only family affected by this disease. We were not alone. Having a plan while dealing with a lot on my plate was a balancing act. But everyone's life gets overwhelming from time to time. So, like most college students, I was up until 2am doing homework, studying, and doing papers. Knowing that all this was worthwhile, once I finished college I would get an excellent job. Finally, I would have a career. My love for helping people was my passion, so my dream job was to work in public service. Since the office where I go is just a nightmare; where they are rude, they make you wait all day for a bunch of nothing, while they treat you like a number, and not a person. They dehumanize you and fail to realize it could be them in this line at any time in their lives. How would they like to be treated?

So, I can help because of my experiences in which I can understand the issues firsthand of people who come to the offices. That is what they need is someone who understands with compassion.

I had to remain strong at all levels and prepare myself emotionally for the blows. Then I had to deal with Michael and his emotions and feelings of going through the experience. This undoubtedly was one of the hardest things about being a parent to a child with such a condition and no cure. Then on the positive, we had to enjoy life in-between. There was hope that a cure would be found, but it was hard to accept the fate he was handed. Acceptance is harder for the parent(s) than the child. Many moments are spent fighting this disease but there has to be a will to live. Once that is gone, then the fight is over no matter how hard a parent fights. Michael was not at that point, but he too has to just live in the moment, not the future that is uncertain in his favor. So, for one child, Ashley, I could look to the future, while the other child was an entirely different story. This was our world.

So, to the MDA doctor again we went. Michael was getting weaker and there was nothing to stop it. As a mother, you're supposed to protect your child from everything, but I can't do anything about this thing he has. I felt powerless. Michael was just approved for a power wheelchair, and he is so excited. His eyes lit up and that smile was contagious. I was excited to see him happy about his new wheels. As options were limited with this condition, Megan's family had struggles as most do to understand what it really was like. When nothing can be done for Michael to their liking, I always have Megan and her parents telling me what decisions to make. They always seem to have all the answers. They have no clue what Michael really has nor what I am going through as a mother. I am so sick of them telling me what I need to do when they just don't know. I had to educate myself on Michael's condition, so that I knew what I was dealing with. Man, by the time I read everything I sounded like a doctor.

This condition is caused by a change in the dystrophin gene. Lack of dystrophin causes muscles to not able to function or repair themselves properly. They become fragile and easily damaged. It is caused by a mutation in the gene that encodes for dystrophin, a protein that is essential to the proper functioning of our muscles. With it, muscles are not able to function or repair themselves properly. The loss of muscle then results in a loss of strength and function.

The condition (DMD) is progressive muscle degeneration and weakness. It's a multi-systemic condition, affecting many parts of the body, which results in deterioration of the skeletal, heart, and lung muscles. It starts with the lower body and works its way upward to the rest of the body. Michael's condition was a mutation, and I was not a carrier. After two genetic tests, one was negative for his type and the other was inconclusive. I was a carrier of Cystic Fibrosis, which none of the children inherited. I still felt guilty and blamed myself for his condition. I was a mother, and my child was sick. I had to make sense out of it.

Michael was always so happy and just went along with the flow. Michael was a good kid and most of the time followed all the rules. I never had to raise my voice at him or his sister. I just let him be a kid. All this doctor stuff was overwhelming for him. He just wanted to play video games, watch movies, and read. He loved Harry Potter and Percy Jackson books. His favorite song was Living on A Prayer by Bon Jovi. This song was perfect for his life and battle. Each day he lived really was a blessing and answered prayer. It could not have been easy to deal with the loss of abilities. This was all taken by the age of six. As he lost the abilities one by one, he would waddle walk, then he crawled, he scooted, and rolled himself around. When all that failed, he was pulled from his legs by Ashley at his request, of course. But he got around and never complained. Blessed with a was a very gentle soul, he never lost touch with how much he loved his sister and mommy.

Michael and Ashley loved attending school; however, Ashley had troubles in school socially which affected her academically. I always thought the issue would get better and the students would learn to just accept her. That never happened. Ashley's brown skin often left her without any friends and racial bullying. Children in her class would claim it was Ashley being sensitive and wanting special treatment because she was, "Black." Comments like, "You know how they are? Maybe they should not have adopted those children." When the parents of these children were called out on their behavior, they got defensive and insisted upon saying once again, "I have Black friends." Really? What does that have to do with anything. Ashley is maybe sensitive to the unintelligent things people say to her and think that these comments are okay to say. Maybe they should just keep their mouth shut. No comments always equal more peace.

On a positive note, they were treated equally when they both would get homework. While doing their homework, Michael would complain about spelling, (which he hated). He decided to make up some story this year at school to try and get out of this very boring subject. The results and reaction from the school were somewhat interesting. It was quite funny when the school believed it. So, what exactly did my lovely son say? He claimed that he wasn't good at spelling because the Muscular Dystrophy affects that part of the brain. The school was so convinced that I had a tough time getting them to understand that Michael was fooling them. He was just a kid. We all shared a laugh about that which is something we all need to do more often, from time to time.

Michael was happy to receive his first power-chair. It took almost a year to get approved from the insurance. There was always a delay when it came to getting approved for things that he really needed. There must have been some committee meeting, that just felt unfair when deciding to approve things for Michael or other kids like Mike. It is always the child that suffers, and we learned early about the so-called insurance. There were many things that Michael just could not have because the insurance would deny so much. This was crazy that children would have to wait so long to get approved and, in some cases, denied. The denials always lead to an appeal which delayed things even more. His physical therapist at the school was happy to see him finally get his chair. He was happy, but he had more expensive wheels than me. His chair cost over $40,000.

Things stayed the same with Michael through Halloween, Thanksgiving, and Christmas. Megan came to bring the presents and I was able to give some presents back this year. Gale always bought them great gifts and in addition, gave them gift cards. It was nice of the family put a smile on their faces. This year Marlon came with Megan to drop the gifts and after leaving out, I noticed he forgot his hat. So, I opened the door, and I overheard Marlon saying to his sister, something about that we should give back to them. I was taken back by it and figured our gifts weren't good enough for them. No, they were not expensive or anything like that. I guess, the thought did not count. But their mother called to say, thank you and I just let it go. But I remembered what Michael told me about his conversations with them. They were almost asking these downgrading questions which made everyone feel uncomfortable. They really did not have the right to say these things. I didn't realize at the time, but it was wrong. Perhaps I should have said something. But I never did.

## CHAPTER EIGHTEEN

# Roadblocks

In February 2007 Michael went to the MDA, and they gave their normal unwelcome news. But they also were concerned that Michael was losing a lot of weight. He was not eating the amount he used to. They also made him go for a sleep study and have a swallowing test done to make sure there were no issues. Ashley stayed busy with gymnastics by going four days a week now. This kept her out of the house and out of the business of what was going on with Michael. This was a good thing because I was trying to shelter her from knowing too much and being traumatized.

Ashley worked really hard in gymnastics to learn new skills. Ashley loved to condition because she had such strength and found it easy. The other girls on the team found the conditioning hard. She was the only person of color on the team and because of that other girls thought it was okay to make comments about her race. Ashley was told by the other girls on a regular basis that the reason she liked to condition was because she was Black. Why can't she just like to condition, and it has nothing to do with her race or color of her skin. If Ashley did not already feel out of place, they continued by saying, "Look at all the muscle the Black athletes have and that's why they are good at certain sports." The conversation went too far, when the girls said,—"Gymnastics is not for Black girls." Their reasoning was that the Black girls get too much muscle, and you must be short, skinny, and light. I guess they did not hear of Dawes who made three Olympic teams. But where are the coaches in this? Even one of the mothers told me that well, if gymnastics does not work out—Ashley can always do track. "They are always good at that stuff." Who are they? She could not get a break at school or the gym. Why did the color of her skin bother people so much? I wish she didn't have to go through this. But life just rolls on no matter what. What did they think that if they make her feel so unwanted that we will just move away. They better think again, I was stronger than that as her mother. My entire life had been a pattern of not being wanted in foster care. So, I was used to this, and I would use my strength to help Ashley stand her ground. These people don't get to choose who stays or goes.

When the kids did something together it seemed like the racial bullying ceased or was incredibly low grade. Michael and Ashley attended the Spring camp, which they always enjoyed so much. In addition, they were registered for the summer camp, as usual. They always stayed so busy with the camp over the summer, until school started back. I graduated from Harper College in May. Then I started classes at Northeastern Illinois University over the Summer. Michael would attend the MDA camp in June but would miss a week of summer camp. He always had a blast at his MDA camp. He would come home with all kinds of stories about his adventures. The school year ended on Michael's birthday, and they started day camp the next day. Camp kept them so busy and safe while I was at work and school. Michael had the same camp assistant from NWSRA as last year. His name is Steve. He was tall with dark hair and slender. He was so good to Michael, while being cautious, gentle, and so respectful. He was a music major in college, but he really cared about my son. Steve made an impact on Michael's life that was very heartfelt.

The visits from Megan started to slow down--as well as from the rest of the family. Ashley was now on a gymnastics team where she worked out five days a week. Once again, this was a good thing that kept her mind off what was going on. For my graduation, I was given a gift in which I decided to do a road trip to Florida. Manny rented a car and did the driving. So, in July we headed to Disney World for a week. We stayed in the POP Century Hotel and had a wonderful time. I spent a lot of time with the kids which was a great feeling to be so carefree. We took a lot of pictures of our adventures. It was nice to do this trip before it got busy in the fall. The kids would be back at school, and I would still be a full-time student, while working full-time.

In August, I married my best friend, Manny. He wanted a baby of his own. We struggled from the start of our marriage, and I just couldn't figure out what was really going on. Sometimes, people are good as friends, and that is what we should remain. I thought the marriage just needed some work; you know, like the development of a relationship. I bent over backwards to be the perfect wife and mother. At times, I felt taken by my husband; while I was screaming inside, and I was trapped. I tried to speak with him many times about this so-called marriage not resembling one. I knew that even more so after I found out I was pregnant in December with our first child.

I needed more from the marriage than what Manny was willing to give. I needed love from him, but I would have to just accept what I was being given. Maybe someday he will love me, hug me, and hold me that way I needed. I just pushed my feelings aside and decided to fucus on the children and the baby on the way. But I was worried that Manny was so distant. There was something more going on than I knew. He acted like everything was wonderful in our relationship. What world was he living in? It was like there were two Manny's. Again, I just pushed my feelings down and ignored my needs and wants. I just wanted to be a great wife and mother.

Magic was a friend but wasn't at all happy that I was with Manny, because he knew from our conversations that Manny didn't love me. He had great concerns for me and the children. He told me, "That man doesn't love you--this isn't going to work out." He claimed I married Manny because he was a safe choice for a partner. Of course, after the dangerous first relationship with my first husband, who can blame him? Even know he didn't agree with what I was doing--he was a great friend and never turned his back on me. Magic would still write, call, and remain supportive.

The pregnancy was a little difficult because I was having awful morning sickness. I didn't get anything else, so I shouldn't complain too much. Gale wasn't too happy about the pregnancy because I wasn't finished with school and didn't have a decent job. She started to give me a speech about how much everything costs. As if I didn't know. She was using her status to tell me I shouldn't be having a baby, but she could. So, she gets to make the decision for me? I know this wasn't the ideal time to have a baby, but it was my decision—not hers. I did community outreach for a child service agency, which didn't pay much. But I was doing something that had an influence. Something that impacted the families in crisis, abused children, battered women, and foster children. Above all-- Michael and Ashley were so excited about the baby!

## CHAPTER NINETEEN

# Bittersweet Moments

I was pregnant both semesters while in college. I stayed focused and planned to take summer classes until the baby was born. Samantha was born in the summer of 2008. She was a beautiful baby. She had my bright eyes, brown hair, and light skin. I was more prepared for Sam than the other two children: while having everything for the baby, such as a crib, swing, diapers, and clothes. I breastfed for the few weeks I was home. I returned to school and work while attending Roosevelt University in Schaumburg when she was just weeks old. I was sad to leave her, but she was well cared for.

Like I said earlier, Gale wasn't happy about the pregnancy. So, when Sam was born, she even went as far as telling me that the foundation money couldn't be used for daycare costs. She felt that she was going to be taken somehow and must pay for things as she did with Michael and Ashley. The truth is that it never crossed my mind. She was very generous and paid for camps for the children, gymnastics for Ashley and contributed money for me to go to the college. I will always be grateful, but it came at a price. Perhaps, they didn't know they were doing it. But the feeling it gave me was that I was not providing for them because they had more. Their decisions were always like they were better and were coaching me. I was always less than them.

I have not one jealous bone in my body for people who have more than me. Having seen more people with money who are unhappy, makes money of zero importance to me. For people like them, they would jump in to only sample a part of our lives, and to give assistance the way they felt was appropriate. Then they would jump out and I think at some point they didn't know what to do.

It's like they are looking into our lives through a glass but have no idea what it felt like for us. The most compassion was given to Michael with the offset going to me as the mother. Often Ashely was just left out of the compassion package.

But I just wanted to get done with college and get an excellent job, so she wouldn't feel the need to contribute anything. I felt awful about taking anything from them and trust me, this was not planned. Our paths crossed at some point and were affected by this meeting. From there it was just pushed in my face. Perhaps, this was their way of staying in Michael's life. My kids were not deprived by my standards or many others. But for this family to constantly make it out that these kids were deprived was based on their own views. I started to see things differently. There was a change in body language. Michael also often felt ignored at this time. The family had gotten busy with their lives. This is what I worried about for Michael, for someone to give him attention and then just disappear for a while. I am not saying it was on purpose or anything like that. Stuff happens and life does too. Michael continued going to the MDA camp every summer while meeting different camp counselors each year. As I stated many times, he always had a blast. Michael was a shining ray of light and had a matching smile. That was how he got through. Especially on those tough days that were so challenging.

Soon after Michael came home from MDA camp he wasn't feeling well. He looked like he lost some weight over the week he was at camp. He went to the MDA clinic where I was used to hearing all the unwelcome news that one parent can manage. The truth was--I hadn't even heard the worst yet, but I was stressed already. Michael's health condition was causing a lot of issues. He was losing weight, having some breathing complications and his spine was curved. All of this came after his tendon release which made it possible to put on shoes. It seems like everything we try to fix; another just starts to deteriorate. It's the wear and tear that we keep putting a band aid on trying to keep Michael going.

I tried so hard to make sure he blended in with all the norms of his world which included his peers. So, wearing shoes was a chosen choice for Michael. He liked to wear jeans, T-shirts, and red shoes. His favorite color was red. In many ways, he was very normal. If you heard him on the phone, you would never even think he had MD. But in person, the chair just made people think a little too much, I feel. So often, people would just make up things about him. There was nothing wrong with his intellect whatsoever. It was just a physical thing that kept attacking his body. Michael would say, "I really hate this thing." I would respond, "I hate it too." MD was so complicated and showed no mercy.

Michael had so many doctors, pediatricians, cardiologists, pulmonologists, orthopedics, physical therapist, neurologists, occupational therapist, specialized technology therapist, social workers, psychologist, and now a gastro specialist GI doctor. Michael needed a feeding tube. Just another thing we will have to deal with. There was just so much already, and it was overwhelming. Then there was the school stuff which was complicated. His team included teachers, specialists, nurses, physical therapists and many more. Then there was a wheelchair guy called Metro Rehab. All this stuff costs a lot of money. Michael was on a state insurance program for children with special needs. Many kids with the same condition and other similar conditions went through the same protocol. It was a hard, complicated process full of red tape. Getting around the tape was half the battle. Kids who have the condition like Michael don't have the luxury of waiting for the appropriate supplies. No parent asks for a sick child.

## CHAPTER TWENTY

# POSITIVE RESILIENCY

There were a few moments like this, Michael would often come home and say other kids called him a disease. He asked if he was contagious. I would always smile and say, "No, Michael. Remember you are Michael, and you happen to have Muscular Dystrophy. You are not a disease." Then he would zoom off in his chair to resume his activities. His spirit kept him going, even at times that were challenging. He kept his smile and will to live. Many people meet me and say, "I know where he gets his spirit and smile from." I just smile. Many people have no idea what it's like to be going through this as a parent. But I learned over the years going through the tough times in the foster care system of how to push through. I just smile, think positive thoughts, and mask my true feelings.

There was no time for all that. I had to be there for Michael and help Ashley cope--all at the same time. I had to be strong. I had to live up to that title so much. It was a gift to be able to help others in their time of need, but a curse at the same time. Mainly from my few friends and classmates. I was always referred to as the strong one, but what happens when the strong one starts to struggle? I had no one to talk to about how overwhelmed I was feeling. My partner wasn't there for me. Magic was right about Manny, so I just withdrew from him as well. I avoided his calls, which made him so upset and worried. He didn't deserve that, so I would at least have a two-hour conversation once a week on Sundays. I struggled reading his letters because they were so loving and encouraging. He wanted me to open up about how I was truly feeling and warned me not to push the feelings down.

I could mask my feelings from everyone, except for Magic. He knew the art of masking well, so he was well aware of what I was doing. It was just easier to say everything was good. That was the best because people really didn't want honesty—not really. There're always a few people who push you to be open and transparent with them, but then they retreat from the conversation extremely disappointed. So, back to saying everything is good or hanging in there works really well. Magic loved emotion and would get grumpy with me about not being honest with him. Then he would tell me how important it was to spend time with the children and had an important thing about having meals as a family. He would even get emotional about missing that time with them while I was working and going to school.

I was feeling lost in all the pressures of life. I had an image just like everyone does. I learned to just smile. Sometimes just the feeling I get when I smile makes me feel better. It gave me hope even when I thought all was lost, but nothing is completely lost until the end. Right now, there is time to shine the ray of light and to pray for strength and guidance. People get scared of what they don't understand. They don't know what to say, so they just don't try to connect. The responses I always get from people, "You are always so strong." The truth is--while they said that I was screaming inside. But as usual, nothing came out except for a smile.

So, I was there for Michael at the hospital. It was very emotional trying to be so focused on Mike, while all the doctors and nurses were in and out. Then I was trained in how to use the machine for the feeding tube and all the care that went into it. I had to be a mother, doctor, and nurse all at the same time. Then there was Ashley and baby Sam. Michael's aide from camp, Steve, came to the hospital to spend time with him. He was like a big brother to him. Steve was always so nurturing and caring to Michael. Ashley was often distracted from the awful things Michael was going through. Ashley enjoyed her new role of being a big sister. More often, she struggled to understand what was wrong with her brother. All she knew was the condition he had was called MD--nothing more. At this age, she had no clue what his fate would be. To her, he was just her brother who happened to need some help from time to time.

In many ways, having a child like Mike, was like experiencing a health scare that would cause a raddle and then once over, was like it never happened in many ways. It was just another addition to having Muscular Dystrophy and never knowing what was going to happen next. Unfortunately, there was no playbook for the next set of events that will unfold for Michael. It was always a "play it by ear kind of moments."

Michael came home two days after surgery but adjusted well to his new medical toy. Just like all things for Michael, he just accepted it and moved on. Life is too short to sit and linger on things that can be adjusted to fit his quality of life. I didn't linger as a parent--we just moved forward as he went through the normal stages of being a kid. Things weren't perfect, but we made the best out of it. Life doesn't obey the law of perfection or perhaps Muscular Dystrophy doesn't. Conditions like this are just a cause for adjustment to ensure that the quality of life is achieved through positive thinking. Healing the mind and soul is always an inner belief that once achieved--the body will follow. Once the mind continues to find the will to live then it will be achieved. However, once that will be lost--so is life. Michael had the greatest will to live with that ray of light. He was a candle that never went out. I don't ever want the candle to burn out. So, for that reason, I never thought about the end.

The feeding tube was a learning adventure for me--along with all the others we have already experienced. Michael was a good sport about it though. He had a blue pump machine which had to be calibrated every morning before use. Then there was a tube that went from the stomach to the machine. Then there were these bags which I poured the foul-smelling brown formula into. We would get twelve cases delivered every month, so we were told. Then the machine and the clear bag were stored in a little black bag-- that rested on the back of the wheelchair. This is how Michael would get his nutrients.

Once a month, I changed the button which was connected internally into his tummy where everything went. The first time I had to change it—I sort of made a big mess. So, the next time I made sure I had more towels. There was kind of some spit-up that came from the inside that smelled bad. However, the smell went away once I inserted the new one. There was always an adjustment period, which this time was about three weeks and then all was back to normal. Michael went to school with this feeding tube and was monitored by his aide that would help him throughout the day. It was hard for Michael to be just a normal kid with all this medical stuff and his aide always around. Again, he never complained.

One thing that was irritating was the talking that people wanted to do around Michael and myself. Whether it was intentional words or just some insensitive comments, people just had something to say. Everyone just became doctors and advisors overnight. Everyone wanted to give their advice about Michael. I had this classmate at school who seemed nice at first. She felt that I was treated better by the office we worked at while attending Harper College.

But one day when we were talking, she told me that I had to put Michael on a breathing tube (as she called it) when he needed it. I explained that Michael has clearly stated that he didn't want to be on one. She told me later that she wanted to smack me because it wasn't God's intension for him to die. She said that God invented the this as an alternative way to breathe, so that kids like Michael could live longer. It went all wrong when you start to bring science and technology into what God's intentions are for anyone. So now you know what God's intention are? Really? She needed to just leave it alone. She had no idea what I was going through as a parent. She never asked how I was coping, but she decided to just judge. This individual told me so many things, which were shocking to where I could have used that to judge her too. The way she came across in front of people was not how she really was. Then one night, on the phone she asked me to open up to her. So, I did--which was a big mistake. She turned around and said I couldn't have gone through all that because I would be a hundred years old by now. Everything I said was true--I have no reason to lie. I sugarcoat most things I say to protect their feelings. After that, I kept my distance from her until we graduated a month later. She checked in with me a few times, but after that we went our separate ways. Which I think was a good thing.

Things people say are quite unthoughtful and uncaring. An example of that is when a woman, just after Michael was diagnosed had the nerve to tell me that Michael was given this disease because

I had a lack of faith in God. More God stuff where they know his intensions. Wow! God is now giving kids diseases so they can meet their maker before their time. Personally, God and I made peace after I went through having my moments when Michael was first diagnosed with MD. I have even misjudged his intensions at that moment, but why shouldn't I have done that? I was working through the emotions of being given terrible news. I think I reacted the way most people would react. Yes, of course, my strength and faith were being tested. But I went through the stages. I was in shock, and then I plunged into despair. As I accepted what was running through his body; I wanted to just run out to the store to buy a bike, skateboard, and anything else that he may lose the ability to use. After acceptance, I still created hope in my mind because I had to stay strong for Michael, as my son with the condition and his sister who is looking on. But I have accepted that people will say things no matter how little they know or understand.

## CHAPTER TWENTY-ONE

# LIFE HAPPENS

Our house was a busy place all the time. The kids went to school on the bus to the school just down the street. Sam went to day care while I was going to school during the day and working. Her father worked as well, so arranging schedules to quite a duty. He worked the overnight shift. Between all the doctor visits of Michael and Ashley's gymnastics--we were all so busy. Ashley went to gymnastics five days a week--for 4 hours a day at the Mega Gym in Barrington. Michael went to her practices on some of the days. He always made friends fast with some of the boys on the team. Michael was just that ray of energetic sunshine which was contagious to everyone he encountered. But Ashley had to deal with a lot of bullying at school. She learned to accept what was happening to her and stayed quiet at school. At home she was in tears now because it hit a peak. I felt so powerless as the kids started to gang up on her. She was known as the sister of Mr. Wheels-Michael. Ashley lived in the shadow of her brother. But she had frustrations and things she couldn't understand, so it bothered her.

Ashley didn't like the wheelchair accessible van and just wanted a "normal car." We were lucky to have this one and I had to put it in perspective for her to understand. But I knew how she was feeling. We were a special family because of Michael's needs. Sometimes we just couldn't do something because it wasn't wheelchair accessible. Sometimes in the winter we would have to drive around the parking lot trying to park because all the snow was dumped in the extra space made for the ramp in the handicap spot. We needed to let the ramp out for Michael to get out of the car.

Other times, people would borrow someone's handicap sign so they could use the special parking and then there was nowhere to park which caused situations.

Eventually, the officer would catch them. But why don't people just think about what they are doing and how you would feel if someone did that to you? Most people must be in the moment experiencing what you are for them to understand. There were many frustrating moments like that. But I had to help the children cope and move forward with a cheerful outlook. I never linger on things too long. I would use my coping strategies, which I was well groomed on from my foster care days. I always push forward by addressing the problem, finding solutions, and applying them. However, with a child with such a condition--there were things just coming up all too often. So, it got overwhelming from time to time. At this point I just stopped talking to people about his condition because I didn't want to make them sad. I would just say everything was "good." That kept the conversation brief.

Michael had a relatively normal life except for the chore part. He would come home from school and do homework. Michael still hated to do spelling and had logical reasons why he didn't need to do it. Michael also had the rule that there was no television during the school week--which he often protested. They both tried everything to get that rule overturned, but it never was. There were reasons for that rule. Pretty normal stuff—you think?

Michael would dress up for Halloween just like all the kids did with some assistance of course. I loved to take pictures of everything just like most parents. So, I would make all three of them pose, so I could get my pictures before they went trick-or-treating. Things were the same each year for the holidays. For Thanksgiving, I made the big dinner with the turkey and all the trimmings. The kids were out the entire week, while I only got the two days from work. I spent those four days with the children watching movies and doing activities. The day after Thanksgiving, we would set up the tree and decorate the entire house.

Megan would always bring presents or gift cards for the children before they would go on their family vacation. Ever since the first negative comments came about the presents and the value of our gifts compared to theirs; I have really distanced myself making our family unavailable to avoid issues.

Christmas Day was always a wonderful time for the kids. We all got to spend time together. They got some presents and stockings with candy. They were always so happy with what they got. They would both say, "This is what I always wanted." That's great! The children were not spoiled, greedy and never complained about anything. As I watched them open their gifts, I realized like I always do; that they were all growing up so fast. This was Sam's first Christmas, so it was special. For a moment, I thought of how many more would Michael have with his sisters? Then I quickly pushed it out of my head to just enjoy the moment. As the year ended, I was hopeful for 2009 to bring great positive things our way. Perhaps a cure for Duchenne's Muscular Dystrophy would be nice.

I always am in a constant battle within between a miracle from God and a cure from science. My faith is always on the focus of getting that miracle, but there are many boys affected by this disease. How would God decide on who gets the miracle and who doesn't. To make it fair--God should just give a miracle to all of them. Wishful thinking? But then there are scientists that are looking for a cure. The MDA puts forth the money from the telethons every year in hope of finding that cure. But I just hope it will happen soon. I have great hope and faith that something will be found soon for this life-threatening disease.

Michael was having a lot of weakness. He started to have a lot of issues with his upper body, losing balance in the chest, and upper shoulders. Michael now started to have a challenging time bringing his hand up to control while using his wheelchair. Most of the year, Michael stayed pretty much the same health wise with these new weaknesses. He was pretty used to losing abilities by now. Besides from all doctor appointments, physical therapy, and other appointments--there were constant adjustments with his IES based on these changing needs. So, he wore AFOs on his legs and a brace around the back to help prevent scoliosis. Then he had all his work on the laptop and didn't use books much at all. But he had his blue backpack on the back of his wheelchair. Michael loved to read all his books from his laptop. He didn't let anything stand in the way of him learning new things.

Michael was used to all these adjustments by now, as this was part of his ever-changing life. He was a happy kid and never complained. Recently, he mentioned that Megan and the family didn't come over as much to visit. He accepted they were busy with their lives and that they moved on to other things. Life keeps moving. But Michael at times felt like they didn't care and forgot about him but took it in stride. He didn't linger on things--just like me.

He had friends at school, so he always had kids to talk to. Michael was a friendly kid who made friends very quickly and that remained the case. The other kids just loved him. I was happy that Michael didn't face any discrimination due to his condition. The kids went to spring camp for a week where they would go on trips every day. Then over the summer they both went to summer day camp at Salt Creek, where they have been going to since 2005. Once again, Michael would miss a week to go to the MDA camp. Ashley went to camp every day and gymnastics after that. They both stayed busy over the summer. I attended classes and worked. The summer was very calm and relaxing with no serious issues with Michael. The Summer always went by so fast and were back in school. I would spend time with the kids on the weekend going to the park, movies, and Twin Lakes. For Halloween, the kids went out--Michael was spiderman and Ashley was a witch. It was a nice night with the kids. We had a special tradition on Halloween after we went out for candy, then we would return home for pizza and movies. We did this every year, and it was a blast!

## CHAPTER TWENTY-TWO

# REALITY BITES

During Winter break, Michael started to have an issue with breathing. He was taken to Lutheran General Hospital which was like his second home. They knew our family well. Michael was diagnosed with chronic Asthma. So, a nebulizer was ordered with medication for him to use at home. He also had inhalers that he had to take every day. Michael was also given the pneumonia vaccination because he was at risk due to his condition. I stayed at the hospital with Mike for ten days until he was released home. When Michael gets sick everything must be arranged according to his needs. The one who suffers is Ashley who gets abandoned in many ways. Usually, I would go to her practice and study while she was at the gym. I supported her as much as one could, but when Michael ends up in the hospital--things just stop.

Ashley's meets and practices would be missed. She would do gymnastics in the halls of the hospital. Sometimes Ashley felt so alone, but understood Michael had special needs. All of this was complicated for her, but it was better for her to be away from all of this at the gym. She already knew so much medical terminology from being around all of this from time to time. The nurses and doctors were all so nice to explain things. The volunteers were always so kind to hang out with Michael and Ashley in the playroom-- to give them normal kid time.

The many feelings I have about Michael having this thing-- which is what I call it, is overwhelming. Michael referred to it as the same and this thing was so annoying. Even when you thought he was doing so well, there was always something lurking in his little body. His body would ache and bother him, but he kept his smile. He was just so upbeat which helped him with his outlook on the condition and life. Michael's room on the other hand was starting to look like a hospital room, which we all just got used to.

Sam would come to visit Michael in his room, and he enjoyed the companionship so much with his baby sister. They would talk about all sorts of things, like books, Legos, and Harry Potter. She had a lot of energy. When Ashley was home, she would hang out with Mike as well. They were close to one another. All of the children were very pleasant and had great positive attitudes. However, Ashley spent many hours at the gym working out. Gymnastics took up most of her time and she enjoyed it. She struggled to make friends and stayed mostly to herself. Ashley didn't like attention from people, but she had no choice but to except the attention that came from her big brother. She loved her brother so much; she was always giving him lots of hugs and it was sweet to see. In return, he would go to her meets. She felt a little embarrassed by the attention.

The year 2010 started out great! Michael was doing well, but then there was some unwelcome news. In March, Dr. Kame said that he needed to see a Spinal Orthopedic Specialist. A month later, we went to The Bone and Joint Institute of Illinois and waited in a room for almost three hours until a doctor came through the door. Dr. Bone, (not name-sorry can't give you that). I never really give descriptions of the doctors because there are so many of them and they keep changing. Their specialty is more important and what they did for him battling this disease is even more so. But unfortunately, doctors are not gods, even if some of them try to have this, "God Complex." They do not know everything, even if some doctors pretend to act in this manner. The real thought is that doctors get frustrated in their profession, especially when there is no cure, and the treatments are limited. These I refer to as the no hope conditions and the let's pray about it. As a parent of a terminally ill child, I had to accept all of this. We do what is scientifically possible and leave everything else up to faith and hope. This was one of those moments of faith and hope. Michael needed spinal surgery for his newest condition of Scoliosis. His spine was so curved that it was now causing some other health issues. We planned the surgery for November 2010. I had to request the time off, so I could be there to take care of Mike. Also, it wasn't considered a right-now surgery, so I wanted to let him have his summer to have fun.

In May, I graduated from Roosevelt University with my BA in Psychology. I graduated with honors and was inducted in the Franklin Honor Society. This was an exciting day. Michael and Ashley came to see my graduation--which was downtown. Gale came in support but had to rush off as soon as graduation was over. It was nice for her to come out. Once you live in the suburbs you forget just how many people live downtown Chicago. It seemed a little bit overwhelming, and just wanted to get home. Now that I had my four-year degree and only six classes away from getting my Graduate degree, I started applying for jobs. I was hopeful of a career now and not just a job, as I have now. So, I applied for a job with the State of Illinois--DHS. This was the job I really wanted. Since I love to help people and had been on the other side, this would be a great fit.

Over the summer the kids did the same as usual. It was all about camp and gymnastics for Ash. For Michael, it was the summer camp and the MDA camp. These activities kept them busy, and they never complained about going. Sam also had fun over the summer with her daycare being run like a camp. I started some online classes for the MA Psychology program and was given a scholarship because of graduating with honors. It was great to get this opportunity to further my education. I really wanted to have a distinguished career in Social Services, of some sort. I have so much to offer with all my experiences of living in a dysfunctional home, being a foster child, domestic marriage, and having a child with special needs. One day, this will happen; I must keep my head up and stay positive.

I needed much inspiration and motivation, so I got just that when I saw the inspirational movie called, "Extraordinary Measures." It is about a father of two children who have a life-threatening disease. He teams up with a doctor to find a cure or treatment before it's too late. The father brings together the entire community of parents and children that are being affected by the same disease as his children.

The movie was based on the book, "The Cure." At the end of the movie, his daughter is riding in the front seat of the car, enjoying freedom. The wind is blowing in her face, and she is happy. The movie gave me hope and inspired me as a parent who is in the same situation. I pray each and every day for a cure before it's too late.

So, here we are with Michael--going through, another major surgery. He was admitted to his second home, Lutheran General Hospital. As a family, we were given this little room to hang out during the surgery. There was a pager given to us so we would know when his surgery was over. So, we spent time together in the room for a while, then I took a walk all around the hospital, and went to the library to get some books. I tried anything to help with my anxiety and had learned a few tricks over the years. After a couple of hours, Manny left the hospital to go back to the house. He claimed he was going to get Sam from daycare early, but honestly, he never liked the hospital thing. Who really does? This is our life.

Shortly before, I found out that I was pregnant and was experiencing a lot of morning sickness. This was a total shock as this was not planned. The babies, (yep twins) due in April, so I was still having a lot of morning sickness. I was praying it would go away soon. So, being at the hospital was hard with all the smells. Finally, after sixteen hours Michael was out of surgery. The norm was the doctor came in and explained how the surgery went. From what they said, everything went well, but he still had that breathing tube. There is always a chance that the breathing tube could be a permanent thing for Mike after any surgery, like this one. Soon after, I was taken upstairs to the peds ICU located in the new tower. My heart was racing as I was on my journey to his room. When I walked in, nurses were working with him. They were hooking up wires for the machines and trying to make him feel comfortable. As I came closer to him, he said, "Hi Mommy." Those are always sweet words to hear from him, especially after a surgery like this. He was a trooper but was all swollen in the face and looked so exhausted. There were so many monitors and two IVs in him. He just didn't look like my Michael, and I pray that he will heal fast.

The staff was always so nice here. They offered me some food now and always asked if I needed anything to let them know. I made the bed up near the window. Afterwards, I went to take a shower and came back to the room to get some rest. Who am I kidding, no one ever gets much rest in the hospital. The room was cold, so I just snuggled under the blankets. I got up several times during the night as the nurses came in to do his vitals, which was every hour. I don't know how any patient gets any sleep at the hospital. So, with all of this, I was exhausted in the morning as I ran to the restroom to deal with the morning sickness. After I arrived back to the room Michael was awake and wanted to talk. He couldn't because he had the breathing tube in, so I was given a book full of titles and pictures of movies. Michael picked out a few, so the volunteer went to get them. After that, the nurses and several doctors came in like an army to give me the status on Mike. They told me all the therapies he would need along with all the care. They said that tomorrow they would remove the breathing tube. However, they warned me that he might have lost the ability to breathe on his own. This means that he would need a CPAP machine or a trach breathing tube.

I was hoping that would not be the case. I don't think either of us were prepared for that. Also, Michael didn't want to be on any machine to help him breathe. This topic would be a difficult and controversial one. Everyone wants to be a parent or doctor when it comes to Mike. Regardless, of having to be the one to care for him. Megan and her family wanted to be drop-in friends. You know the ones who pop in and out of his life, but never really understand the feelings to the total situation. I needed them to be impartial, but they had some issues there. I understand the kids spending time with Michael and just being there for him. Which stopped unless he was in the hospital But, the parents never really asked me, How I was doing? They kept their feelings hidden or were too busy trying to fix everything. It's vastly different from the drop of compassion that was absent. They just didn't get it.

## CHAPTER TWENTY-THREE

# Positive Hopes

The next day, the breathing tube was removed, and Michael started to struggle. He was put on a CPAP machine. Cardiology and Pulmonology were called to the room to help stabilize his heart and lungs. They were all working on him, and I was looking on from the side of the room. It looked serious and thoughts started racing through my head. Was this it? Why did I agree to this surgery? Did he really need it? Then it happened--a code blue was called. I was removed from the room. The chaplain arrived and just sat there with me. I thought, this was it. With a child with Muscular Dystrophy--you always have in the back or your mind...what would be the moment that would take him away from this world?

Then comes all the emotions, like sadness, anger, fear, and grief. All the emotions come pouring through, even the ones that you push deep down. On a day-to-day basis, you think positively and remain with plenty of optimism and faith. But at moments like this, all of that is tested because you know what this disease can do. This disease is so unfair. I swear if I had a dartboard at home for every time something health wise went wrong, it would be filled up. Sometimes, ignorance is bliss.

After an hour, a doctor came out and approached me. As he moved closer to me, all those thoughts came racing once again. Was he coming to tell me the famous line, "Sorry we have done everything we could possibly do, but despite our efforts, he passed away?" Even the people in white--the doctors don't know all. But, from their prospective losing a patient so young could never be an easy conversation.

As I looked down the hallway, I could visualize the scene in the movie, The City of Angels, where Nicolas Cage takes the little girl by the hand, to meet her maker. Sometimes when life doesn't make any sense, a song, a book, or movie can help ease the pain I was feeling.

All the prayers I had said must have helped. See, I told you me and God are on good terms. Or Michael was going to be the newest Angel up in heaven. I was given the news, Michael was stable. He was on a CPAP machine along with all of this. His room looked like a medical nightmare with all these machines, tubes, and wires. But on the other side, perhaps Mike got a miracle and God pulled him through.

Doctors didn't think he would recover breathing on his own. I still had hope that he would recover. He was on this loud CPAP machine that was pushing air into his lungs with a mask which he had to wear 24 hours a day. Occasionally, he could have if off for a while. Especially when his sister Ashley came to visit him. They would talk some before Michael would have some other treatment. After that, she would do gymnastics in the hallways, while Michael would talk to me and use his laptop to communicate. He loved to watch movies and have some visitors. Megan and her family came at separate times to visit Michael. He looked happy to have the visits from them. When I got to the hospital from work, they would share some words with me and leave soon after. Then it was just Michael and me. Manny tried to keep Sam away from the room because she would be somewhat noisy.

After a week of being there, Michael developed fluid on the right side of his lungs causing more health issues. Megan's mother Gale was at the hospital visiting with me when Michael started to struggle a bit. Then she just said, "bye." She headed for the door and was gone. That really bothered me--I thought she was a friend. How could she just walk out? I felt so alone with all this stuff going on with Michael. This is the loneliness I had to deal with while having no one to talk to. So, I kept my feelings all bottled up and felt it was best that way.

A code blue was called for a child in the next room, a girl battling cancer. When any code blue was called, a cold chill ran down my back. Some of the parents from the other rooms would peek out with concerned faces. All our kids are in ICU--at any time could just slip away. You never know. I didn't want to peek out because I knew what that mother must be going through. Later, I walked past the girl's room. I saw the chaplain in the room--with the parents, I think. The bed was covered by a sheet. I saw more family members in the room where families can spend time together. There were about twenty people all crying and hugging each other. The little girl, named Angel, died. It was so sad, and I was too overwhelmed with emotion, so I went into the restroom to cry. It's just not fair.

That same night, Michael told me about his dream he had. When Michael stopped breathing and a code blue was called, he was in a cloud in the sky. He met a man there with dark hair and dressed in white with wings. The man spoke to him, but he didn't remember what he had said. So, the man took him by the hand where they ended up in the hospital room. Michael looked up and the man was next to him on the bed. After that he closed his eyes. Then when he woke up, the man was gone. But he claims to have seen this man every day in his room. When he was telling me this, I knew it wasn't a dream. While he was down, he had an out of body experience. He saw an angel who brought him back. It wasn't his time. Michael named the man, Magic. I just looked up when he said that because I have a friend named Magic. I have never told the kids I called Magic, well Magic. I called him by his real name when I took the kids to see him for a visit. The kids knew him by his real name only. So, I guess we have another Magic! In times like this, I really need an angel.

Michael spent another week in the hospital and then could go home. He recovered and was able to breathe on his own. But his lungs suffered badly. He needed a vest to be worn twice a day that would shake him, so the mucus would loosen up. This was to allow him to stay clear. Then the doctors, who never had any good news, said it would only be time before we would have to decide on whether to do a trach breathing tube or not. I was told about some other options, but realistically without one, Michael would just pass away. I am paraphrasing what the doctors said because they can be so dramatic.

I just tried to block everything that they just said out of my head. I wanted to just focus on having this time with Michael because never knowing when his fall from grace will happen is hard. I had so many feelings about all of this, but found when people, especially doctors, would ask about how I was coping; so just to put a smile on my face. I had one friend, Jane, but we didn't talk much, and I told her the same thing; that I didn't want to explain anything. I didn't want the attention or didn't want to bore people with such emotional drama. Again, the loneliness consumed me. I tried to distract myself with my master's studies and work. As much as I pushed it out of my head, the more it came back to haunt me.

## CHAPTER TWENTY-FOUR

# LIFE CHANGES

When Michael came home, there were some adjustments. The major one was that with rods in the back, he couldn't look down. So, everything had to be put up high so that he could see it. So, the television and laptop had to be adjusted. He also felt heavier since the surgery, so, moving Michael was harder. Michael already had a bathing seat and a toilet seat to accommodate his special needs. Manny had to lift him because of me being pregnant. Michael returned to school the following Monday.

I had some fights with the school because they wanted Michael to remain at home longer. I tried to give Michael the same quality of life as the other kids. I think personally, they were just getting scared of all the health stuff going on with him. I totally understand, but he deserves to be around kids his own age. There was no good reason for him to be at home. He wasn't just going to sit at home bored. Michael loved school and was smart, so he deserved to be there. I tried not to visualize beyond grade school in fear that he wouldn't be here with us. I tried to clear my mind and stay in the moment.

In January 2011, I moved Michael a bit on the bed and a few hours later I started to have some complications with the pregnancy. I thought I lost the babies, but I lost one of them. The baby that survived had fetal cardiac surgery at 25 weeks gestation. There could be possibly a kidney issue as well but won't know until she is born. Yes, another girl! So, March 25, 2011, Maddie arrived. She was in the wrong position, so it was thought that I would have to have a C-section. But finally, she dropped down in the correct position and came out. She was born with Craniosynostosis. She had a premature closing of the soft spot that was absent. I just started crying when they told me that she needed to see a Neurosurgeon. I had to take her to Children's Hospital located in Chicago. They did some imaging tests and it confirmed what she had this condition with some fluid on the brain. Surgery was scheduled for when turned eight weeks old. We would have to wait until that time to have the surgery. I was hoping Michael's condition stayed stable while I dealt with Maddie's condition. She already had surgery before she was even born that was very risky. So, this was overwhelming.

So, the day of the surgery we arrived early. It was nerve wrecking, and I was so scared for her. But after three hours, she was out of surgery and in recovery. Maddie looked so helpless. She struggled a little with getting the pain under control, but after that she was taken to her room. Maddie was scheduled to be in for a week but was such a trooper just like her brother Michael. Her doctor suggested putting her in the car seat because they wanted the fluid to drain. She had this water balloon in the back of her head. Two receiving blankets were rolled up and stuck on each side which made it look like bunny ears sticking up. Maddie then rested her head on this little blue donut. The water balloon felt warm and so soft. When the doctors came by the next day, she was just smiling. So, she was doing well, and came home in three days--instead of a week. We had to take some precautions, but otherwise she was going to be okay. Maddie had a follow up with another Ct scan which looked great. I was told because it was done so early, that she would have no issues later. Michael was such a big brother and was so worried about her. He knew all too well about having surgery. Michael was hoping she was not going to need any more surgery. In the future, her head shape should get more rounder. Her head looked like an egg and her forehead was larger than normal. But by age five, everything should normalize.

As sixth grade closed for Ashley, it was obvious she was struggling with dealing with the bullying, Michael's condition, and going to Jr. High. She was desperate for friends which lead to the most unthinkable incident besides the bullying to take place in the library at her school. Two boys violated my daughter in a sexual nature. Certain touching occurred and it happened on more than one occasion. I couldn't believe this took place at a school. Was she safe anywhere? This was a sad moment for my daughter and for myself as a parent. It took some time for her to talk about what happened. Part of the reason that she thought the school would blame her for this was because they did with the other bullying that occurred. This was inappropriate by any means, but not much could be done because they were students. Ashley started treatment and was able to process. She worked through what had happened to an extent, but she would struggle for many years because of what she experienced. After that, she decided she wanted to be homeschooled.

The summer went the same as usual. There was summer camp, MDA camp, and gymnastics. Sam was at daycare for her summer camp and Maddie joined her three days a week. I was studying to get my MA and worked full time. It wasn't a career job, but it was something until I found one. I also wanted to finish my degree program, but Megan couldn't leave alone enough. She came to visit Michael with her brother and started asking personal intrusive questions. Some had to deal with the new baby, my job, and income. The kids told me about the conversation when I arrived home. I was like, really? Like, who are they to be questioning anything. The kids felt bad because Michael knew what they were hinting at concerning the job. I was feeling degraded working at an almost minimum wage job. I won't be there forever and soon I will be done with college completely. Applying for jobs every day was always on my to-do list. Megan felt like just because I had a baby, I wasn't going to have a career. They didn't even know I was getting my graduate degree because I never told them. This came across as like them trying to tear me down and crossing the line. It was wrong to ask the questions to my kids. Some people feel they can do anything if they can get away with it. I was not happy with what took place, but telling their mother was pointless, so I just let it go.

The Fall 2011, the kids went back to school. Michael was in ninth grade at Palatine High School. Ashley was Winston Campus Jr. High. I was attending classes at Roosevelt University and working at Community Outreach. Manny was working at Walmart overnight just down the street from the house. We were all busy juggling schedules for the kids and parenting. I was just praying Michael would stay a bit healthy for the rest of the year.

For Halloween, the kids went to the high school for the big party they throw every year. The children dressed up and had a really enjoyable time, as always. This big party was a week before the 31st, so a little distance between the two candy collecting events. On Halloween, there was a party at school and the trick-or-treating afterwards.

For Thanksgiving, we had the same tradition every year. On Thursday, we had a big dinner, and I spent a lot of time with my children. Then on Friday, we put the tree up with all the decorations. We would play Christmas music which really brought in the spirit. The kids would dance around while Michael would roll around in his chair. He loved being around his sisters and spending time with them. I wanted to remember him just like this--happy, cheerful, and with me. This is where he should be, right? I sat on the couch just watching all of them all having so much fun together. In my deepest thoughts, I would have visions of losing Michael. Then I would take a deep breath, while closing my eyes, and then there would only be my girls. Then Michael would zoom over to me with his chair, "Mommy, I love you." He said, in an incredibly cheerful voice. That was my Michael, always happy, in a great mood, and ready to live each day no matter what. He was a remarkable son, human being, and brother. Many could learn a lot from him.

Our year ended with Michael staying healthy. We didn't have any holiday emergency visits to the hospital. We remained at the house for the entire holidays and this year will be the one to remember. As we were traveling down a road with an illness that was unpredictable and relentless, we had to count our blessings of spending time during the holidays at home and not in the hospital.

In January 2012, I took Michael to the MDA like I did every six months. A doctor there said I would have to decide on the trach, and I needed to be prepared for this, but I wasn't ready. That same day, he had a visit with another doctor who was more liberal about certain rights that the parents and kids had. It always took me days to recover from the negativity and no hope news given by the all-bad news-doctors. It's incredible what all this negativity took out of me. I felt so defeated and no one understands unless they have been there through the thousands of appointments. But this one doctor said we shouldn't put Michael on a trach, and that we don't want all these holes to become who he is. In addition, the surgeries weaken him, so we better think wisely. The last advice was to not prolong his life and to remember him the way he is now. Maybe he was right?

On the way home I thought about what the doctor said. Withholding medical treatment? Isn't that called euthanasia? Would that be considered murder? Wow! Are these normal thoughts or am I just analyzing a bit? I do tend to do that from time to time. I remember learning about euthanasia and Dr. Death who assisted people with suicides. This happened with people who were terminally ill like Michael. Different countries have different rules on this kind of conduct. Is it really murder if the patient refuses treatment and has lost the will to live? I have always felt that once a person loses the will to live, then it's them making the choice. Michael has made it clear he didn't want to be on any machines to help him deliver any functions, such as breathing or keeping his heart pumping. So, at what age can a terminally ill child make that decision?

The better question is, since we are not the ones in pain and suffering, so who should make that decision? With children, shouldn't the child of age 12, or so be able to make that decision? Some professionals have stated that parents are so busy fighting for their child that they fail to realize the fight is already over. As a mother, I already am thinking of the next treatment that will perhaps prolong the inevitable. There are life threatening diseases and then there is the terminal illness like Duchenne's Muscular Dystrophy where there is no treatment to stop it; just a handful of medications to slow the progression, but nothing more at the time. Some would offer the opinion that individuals suffering shouldn't be able to make decisions to withhold medical treatments to end their suffering. For that argument's sake, should the people who want to prolong someone's life who is suffering be able to make that decision? Both arguments are subjective. I don't think anyone wants to make that call. I will let Michael make that decision and make sure he understands the alternative.

# CHAPTER TWENTY-FIVE

# LIFE ROLLS ON

Michael stayed relatively healthy, which was an incredibly positive thing. This is a moment when nothing major happened, which allowed him to be that normal kid. Michael loved going to school and learning. He was able to make and keep friends very easily. I wish I could say the same about Ashley. I knew that going to Jr. High can be difficult. I think it's the age and everything is changing at the same time. Things were just taking a toll on her and she got overwhelmed. She was a cheerleader now, on the gymnastics team, and a full-time student. Homeschooling was put on the table, but she really wanted to be in school. Ashley started falling apart in January.

One of her teachers implied that she was not trying hard enough and would point her out in front of the entire class. This caused a backlash against her from a lot of the students. There was another student of color in the class who would point out when he was late for class. But it appeared there was special treatment given to the white students she had preference for; and all her students were not treated the same way. Then the teacher decided to compare her to her brilliant brother Michael who she also had in seventh grade. She remarked that she would perform better if she went home and got help from Michael because her teacher didn't have the energy. Ashley's teacher was low energy with no empathy--having just had triplets last year, they had been sick for the last few days. That is not Ashley's problem. While we can have compassion—she was still a history teacher supposed to teach and assist. In short, this abuse went on for a few months until Ashley did something to get even with the teacher.

This incident, as we might call it, caused a string of events to occur, not only for Ashley, but for the teacher, the teacher's friends who she decided to email which became viral—and the principal that was friends with her as well.

For Ashley, it meant constant emotional abuse that turned to mental abuse. Then, the discipline continued for weeks to where it was not communicated what she even did. There was no paperwork for what she was disciplined. I understood what she had done to get even with her teacher and so did Ashley. It was unethical that the principal—who was friends with the teacher who was abusive--never did an investigation. Nothing was ever done about the teacher having some predjustice and discriminatory views that lead to discrimination in the classroom. The other child of color in the classroom left the school soon after this.

The email that went viral had some consequences for the principal that optioned not to return next school year. One of the friends decided to join her. Ashley was removed from the classroom and placed in another. But she was accused of several things that she did not do but was forced to take the blame. Comments were made that were very questionable, but when I brought them to the school board, suddenly the witnesses weren't available or moved away. The other excuse was there was a misunderstanding, so no one was blaming Ashley. Well, then why was she disciplined? When you asked for the incident report suddenly that disappeared too. This was not the first time either. By February, Ashely hated school and started to isolate herself from everyone. By mid-February I removed her from school, and she was homeschooled. Things were completely turned around for the more positive, for Ashley. As one avenue was happy and at peace, another one was starting to fall apart.

Since her bullies could no longer get to her at school, they decided to come to the YMCA gymnastics team gym to cause trouble. As the stresses of these incidents kept occurring, Ashley didn't feel safe there either. Ashley started to internalize what was happening to her by finding negative things to release her feelings. She started to control what she could do in her life such as eating, sleeping, and self-harm. She was offered therapy, but she claimed everything was ok. So, when people say a little bit of teasing does not affect a child—perhaps it's because your child is the one doing the teasing. The problem is when you have a brother with a life-threatening disease, the child who is healthy tries to hide everything that they feel will cause problems. Ashley became the peacekeeper.

During one practice, I got a call from the YMCA that Ashley had collapsed during practice and was taken to the hospital. This is the call no parent wants to receive. When I arrived, she was already awake and doing well. The paramedics left a report that she looked very pale when they arrived, but after they got her into the ambulance, they saw some improvement. Ashley collapsed after the girls were all denied a break based on their performance during practice. This meant no water in an extremely hot gym. This was wrong. The head coach was away at some conference at the time but had a mouthful of negative comments to say about my daughter when she returned. At that point there was talk that they wanted her off the team. Some tests were done at the hospital and then she was released. She went to the hospital for some other tests, including the heart. She was given the all-clear and headed back to the gym. I started looking for a new gym because I knew they were trying to get rid of her.

A few weeks later there was a meeting with the YMCA director and her head coach. The coach stated that Ashley did this to herself by not drinking water. So, she was being kicked off the team because she was dehydrated? Strange punishment, I think. There was something going on behind the scenes. But it was clear that she wasn't wanted. Constant comments about her ethnicity, race, and other comments were overlooked. They could say things to her, but she couldn't say things back. Incredibly sad, that other girls and their mothers could say how she was adopted over and over, but that was, ok?

In March 2012, we were preparing to move her to another gym called Legacy Elite when another incident takes place. Which turned into an attack on the entire family. The coach could have advocated for the entire situation, but she chose not to. So, what happened? During practice, she had a conversation with another gymnast who asked questions about Michael. She said that she hadn't seen Michael and asked if he was, okay? Ashley told her that he had some surgery but is home. Her young teammate then took the question a step further when she asked, was Michael going to die? Ashley said, one day he will, and I will miss him. That girl went and told the entire team that Michael died.

Ashley thought the teammate had told the girls that Michael would eventually lose his battle with the condition. Ashley agreed with that, but later I found out that Ashley agreed that he died already. I had no idea. Where were the coaches while this was going on? No one called me to ask if this was true. Everyone was gathering for this incident, but never called to confirm. The coach really didn't like Ashley, so she let these rumors go on for days.

Then one of the mothers called me, you know the one who has the snotty daughter on the team. She was quite attacking and aggressive on the phone. She was like, *your daughter Ashley went around in the gym and said Michael had died. (Ashley denied this), but the mother insisted that Ashley needed to get some help.* So now she is a psychologist. This was the last straw with the coach. There were many other things that took place including racial discrimination that Ashley had to endure for the four years she was on the team.

There was a meeting before Ashley's departure which seemed a bit out of place. I actually thought the mother called because they found out that Ashley was leaving. But to my surprise during the meeting, they had no idea that she was leaving. The meeting was a cover for the coach who was violating the ethics of coaching. There was talk of the discrimination and the YMCA was reaching out because of this and the fact that they were accusing Ashley of lying by stating her brother had died, when in fact he did not. All the talk was not investigating the situation, but they had already taken sides and weren't trying to be supportive.

I didn't sense them being real, but just trying to cover up the fact that Ashley collapsed because of their coaching methods. There was liability and they needed to get rid of her. I took one look at the coach and said we already had plans to leave before this incident took place. That is what she shared with her teammate who went to mouth the inaccurate information, but never said what was really stated or the fact Ashley was leaving the team. So strange what she decided to share. Much more came out after she left the team which caused parents to take sides in the entire ordeal. This incident would follow Ashley for years to come, little did we know at the time. She left with another gymnast, named Jenny. We decided to carpool with the family. This seemed like a good deal.

Ashley loved her new gym and the coaches treated everyone very fairly. The coaches saw my daughter had great strength. Her friend Jenny had great flexibility but revealed that she hated gymnastics. I was a bit shocked that she felt like that, and she wanted to quit. Her parents would not let her do that, so she was stuck. Ashley went to the gym five days a week, and this was her outlet for all the stresses in her life. Here, she was accepted, and she felt like it was family. Ashley didn't have to worry about the bullying and Michael so much. She could actually free herself while she owned her talent at the gym.

As school came to a close, Ashley finished seventh grade by the method of homeschooling, which she loved. We didn't know if she would be home schooled next year or return to school for eighth grade. We decided to take one day at a time. Michael would be going to 10th grade at high school. Like every year, I had a meeting for Michael for the impending school year. He attended these meeting and was always giving his opinions. I loved the insight my son contributed. I would be thinking about it, he would give me this look, then I would tell him to just say it. Michael would look at his aid and just smile. After that, very politely he would start talking.

Michael and I were always so close because we connected on the intellectual, political, and psychological levels. This was different from how I connected with Ashley. Michael and I would have some long enthusiastic discussions that included theology. I valued every moment that we shared together discussing subjects. I loved having that bond with him alongside being his mother. Life is short. In our case, it was even shorter unless they found a treatment for this relentless disease. I, like all parents who have a child with a life-threatening-terminal illness, could only pray.

Summer was a peaceful time for the kids. Sam and Maddie went to day camp over the summer. Michael went to the MDA camp for a week. This would be the last time Michael would be heathy enough to attend. Ashley continued gymnastics over the summer, as in this sport, there was no off time. She would go to the pool in the back of the condominium to swim after practice. Michael's health remained kind of stable, but as always, even when you think everything is ok--the disease is still attacking. You must always hope for the best and be prepared for the worst.

The summer remained very peaceful, which was a great blessing for our family. Megan and her family didn't seem to visit much anymore. Everyone's lives get busy to where things start to change. The once close friendship and priorities had shifted to call me if something serious happens. Little did we know that Michael was going to take a turn for the worse. However, did I really want Megan and her family here? Would Michael want people who had seen him in such positive happy moments to be there around him when things aren't so happy and exceedingly difficult? Were they prepared for these moments? People sometimes are glad to be there when things are good, but struggle when things go bad. How could they understand what Michael was going through? How could they understand what I was going through as a mother? Then there was Ashley…they didn't have a clue.

They had these so-called perfect lives where their concerns could not even compare to the looking glass of the lives that they attempted to help. The problems that were out there were filled with more people like us, and less people like them. I know they had good intentions, but even the greatest people with those same aims could not comprehend what it is like to be us. On the other hand, we cannot judge them because they have contributed positive things--materialistic and financial--but that is what they can offer. The possibility to understand, give compassion, and be a friend to lean on emotionally was just not there. That looking glass went both ways, so this I understood and accepted.

In the Fall 2012, school started as usual. Michael was in 10th grade now. Ashley was back in school for eighth grade for a half-day. The new principal made it clear that he would not tolerate any sort of bullying. Ashley decided to try it. Sam started preschool at Conyers. We weren't prepared for what was about to happen with Michael next.

On September 10th, 2012, I got a call from the school that Michael didn't look good and asked for me to come in. On the way, I picked up Ashley just in case we ended up at the hospital. When I got to Michael's school, I saw an ambulance in the front. As soon as I walked in, the security officer escorted me to where Michael was. Manny stayed with Ashley in the van. I thought I was just going to pick him up and take him home, but that wasn't the case.

He was having some heart issue, and he was taken to Northwest Community Hospital. I rode with Michael, and he was talking just like normal. After arriving at the hospital, he was seen by numerous doctors where you had to repeat everything every time someone new entered the room. All the time I was talking with them, I had this bad feeling that Michael was having some significant issue; however, I had to do the press conference, which was so annoying. They finally hooked him up to a monitor and gave him an IV. Finding a line for Michael was hard because he was so boney. Everything made a bruise on him no matter what. They ran some tests, took some blood—'the vampires' as Michael called them. Then, the medical team asked some more questions about his condition.

All the time I was thinking, shouldn't they know about this condition and what it does to these boys? Unfortunately, some doctors know more about this condition than others. So, as I have found out, doctors aren't gods. Most of the doctors that have worked with Mike don't have that "I am god complex." So, they performed a procedure and gave him some meds for the heart issue without the knowledge of the Duchenne's. They arranged for a pediatric emergency team to come and escort Michael to Lutheran General Hospital. Michael seemed in good spirits after the medication. He started talking to his nurses and doctors about what he likes and his interests. He would go on and on about these things. I knew as his mother what he liked. Michael loved CSI, Myth Busters, and Conan. He loved these kinds of shows and a few others, like The Big Bang Theory and Law and Order: SVU. He also loved Stephen Hawking and saw him as aspirational because of his illness that was said to bar him from living life. Michael loved to read Harry Potter, Percy Jackson, and anything sci-fi. He also loved to play video and computer games. Michael had some issues with his hands, but he still managed to play them. He loved Conan so much and would tell me all about the shows. Sometimes I would watch it with him, but he surely would fill me in when I missed the show with him. We had numerous conversations about them. Most of all, he loved life and each day he was given that opportunity. When your days are limited, you see things differently than when your life doesn't have a time limit.

At the hospital, Michael looked over at the chair. I looked over at the same chair and then back at Michael. He said there was a man sitting there smiling. Michael called him Gabe and said he was an angel that was always with him, even at the hospital. He was even there in the morning when he woke up. I just smiled as he told me all about this angel, and then Michael spoke of another angel. The second angel sounded different--not like a guardian angel--but perhaps one who was there for another purpose altogether. What that purpose was kind of scared me. I saw movies and read about guardian angels and then there was mention of the Angel of Death. I was told that angels surround sick children, and they are always present. I also had this mythical thought that he would be here to take Michael to heaven. I was hoping his time was not now.

The team arrived from Lutheran General Hospital and loaded him into the transport. We started on our way and Michael was in the back just talking about all his favorite shows. I was in the front with the driver. There were no sirens, which took the excitement away. It was rush hour, so there was a lot of traffic. At some point things changed. Michael stared to struggle, so the guy in back said, "light it up." Which meant turning on the sirens because Michael was in trouble. The driver tried to calm me, but I kept looking in back. I knew something was wrong. We got to the hospital and Michael was in the ICU room, two doors down from where he was before. The doctors rushed in, and I went back into a corner near the window.

I saw a bright shining light coming from the ceiling and directly landing on Michael. Was this a sign? I was moved out of the room and was standing behind the door. A doctor was speaking with me trying to find out what the other hospital had done. Then the code blue was called. The doctor I was talking to, and a few others ran towards his room. A mother from another room next door--just looked at me with such compassion. Then Michael's pulmonary doctor and nurse ran towards his room. When he saw me, he said, "It's Michael?" I said, "Yes." Michael was in cardiac arrest.

I was led over to the bad newsroom as I called it. It was a room next to the tower patio which was the only place to get a signal for the phone. The chaplain was called. I told them if Michael went down three times, don't try anymore. I signed a DNR a year ago, but it was void. I thought in a situation like this that I'd know what I don't want and what Michael would want, but I didn't. At that moment, I went blank and went into save Michael mode, no matter what. I couldn't bear life without him. I couldn't lose my Michael. I felt a touch on my shoulder, but when I turned around, nobody was there. I felt at that moment, as the chaplain was saying a prayer and trying to give me hope--that I needed an angel. I noticed she didn't tell me that he was going to be all right. I think she knew. I decided to call Gale and let her know what was happening.

An hour later, a doctor came out and told me that Michael was stable, with a breathing tube. However, his heart was in and out of a dangerous arrhythmia. Michael's heart was in the upper 180s. He needed surgery, but he was too weak. They wanted to put a pacemaker in. Then, the talk about a trach was brought up again. I told them I would think about it. So much goes through your head, as they rushed me to decide. I just couldn't do it. I went into the room to see him, and he was covered in tubes and machines. This was my little boy, Michael.

I noticed the light was still glaring on him. I just sat down on the couch in the room and started crying. I was being forced to make the decision that could ultimately be the end of Michael. He would be no more. Little did I know, Gale, Megan, Manny, and Ashley were in that room right outside the unit. Gale says, "Everything is downhill from here." When I heard she said that I was like, "Who gives her the right to decide that?" Everyone is the doctor, and everyone wants to play God. Sometimes people have to learn what to say and when to say it or when you should just remain silent. I just wanted the world to just stop for a moment, so I could rewind and have my little boy back.

I wanted to go back to when he was a baby and before all this. During the day you can pretend everything is all right. You can fool people and yourself. You can wear a mask, but, at night, you must deal with your feelings in the dark while your loneliness just eats at you. All your sorrows, pain, and regrets just eat you alive. I felt so alone in all of this. My husband couldn't even connect with me to even understand that his antisocial behavior wasn't what I needed. I needed to be hugged and I needed him to be there to connect on an emotional level. Unfortunately, I got nothing other than "You are strong." Megan's family came to see Michael during the times I wasn't there and had to work and attend classes online. One week later, I spoke with Michael about the pacemaker and trach. Michael was using a CPAP machine currently. He could not breathe naturally, and he still needed assistance, but doctors didn't think he was going to recover this time. Michael told me that they were talking with him about the trach that I had to decide about. I really didn't want them to be involved in this decision. More like too many hands in the cookie jar effect. Michael said they initiated the conversation about it. I want to think it was all in good faith and them trying to be there for him. However, Michael felt that they wanted him to get the trach, or they would be mad. I told him, it was his choice, and nobody will mad.

I had to tell him the awful truth--you get the CPAP or the trach and the pacemaker, but there was nothing else that could help him. He would only have a few months on the CPAP, and he would be homebound. He would have more time with the trach but would need a nurse. Michael had state insurance and it would have to be approved. This insurance made things so complicated to have home nursing, an agency would come out to the hospital and do an eligibility interview and then we would have to wait to see if he were approved. Then, I must see what hours a nurse can be at the house. My husband and I both work and I have online classes and I only have one semester left. Ashley still has her gymnastics, and I can't ask her to quit. I didn't want her to resent Michael being sick. This was all difficult and stressful. If Michael chooses not to have any further treatment, this will mean the end for Michael.

# CHAPTER TWENTY-SIX

## Unfair Uncertainties

After much thinking and talking to Michael, he was just as scared as I was. He didn't want to leave his family, but there were no alternatives. Michael didn't want to die, so we chose to prolong his life with machines. Michael had hope that a treatment could be found before it's too late. Positive thinking is a great gift, but a miracle from God was a better chance. Why would any child choose to die? He was in so much pain--but chose the pain over what God had originally planned for him. Where is the faith in that? People built machines to prolong life. Whose plan do you follow? Where do you draw the line?

By Halloween 2012, Michael had the trach surgery and on November 12, 2012, he had pacemaker surgery. To put it in perspective, as the doctors explained, they put a hole in my child's throat. Doctors want to give such a visual. Would they want that visual if it was their kid? I had to push that thought out of my head with all the unpleasant thoughts these doctors and other people put there. Michael went through weeks of therapy with the trach. There are all sorts of cuffs that had to be tried on so that Michael could talk. Then there was the training for the trach, with all the suctioning and care that went into it. I had to learn to change the pieces just in case the nurse wasn't there.

There was an oxygen machine/monitor, blood pressure machine, and so many medical supplies that Michael's small little room would look like a mini hospital. He even was to get a hospital bed and IV pole. Then there were the oxygen tanks just in case we had to put him on oxygen. There were so many changes and preparations to bring him home. Nursing was set up and a nurse was going to come and meet with me at the hospital. They were amazed at how Michael never had a nurse until now. So, as a family we would care for Michael and the nurse would be there for 12 hours a day. She would travel to school with him and care for him throughout the day. His school staff were incredibly good to him and visited home almost once a week.

So, on January 12, 2013, Michael came home from the hospital. This time the transition was a bit tough. The girls were prepped for the nurse that Michael would have. Janet would be here for the week and Dawn would be here on the weekends. Janet was nice and had patience. She would explain things to the girls when they had questions. But Dawn, oh boy. She was a pain and had too much personal stuff going on. She would tell Michael all about her personal stuff including some custody battle her son was having with the ex. I had to explain to her that we didn't need to hear about all that. Certain things just needed to remain private. She was annoying. Didn't she understand, Michael was having the battle of his life?

Things were difficult with Michael's health condition getting worse all the time. Having in-home nurses sounded great at first, but quickly turned into drama. Whenever one of the nurses couldn't come in--I would miss work. Things were complicated when this did occur. The weekend nurse did this almost every other weekend. There was no back up nurse. Michael had to have care on a 24-hour basis. While I was making dinner, Ashley would stay in the room with Michael and assist him. Sometimes, the formula for his feeding tube would make him sick and he would have to throw up. So, Ashley would hold the bucket so he could take care of business. Then he would sometimes complain about something she did. I would remind Michael, "What sister would hold your puke bucket?"

He was a lucky kid to have so much help from Ashley and Sam. A few minutes later, he would apologize to Ashley, and all would be forgiven. Even though Michael had this MD thing, they would still argue with each other, especially with Ashley. They had a joke; Michael would tell Ashley that she stole all his muscle because she was so muscular from gymnastics and he wanted it back. Michael needed distractions like that a few times a week.

Over the rest of the school year, Michael would end up in the hospital three times with respiratory infections. Again, everything would stop. Then his nurse Janet would try to be at the hospital, which wasn't allowed. She would try to play rank, but the hospital had to have a nurse that was from the hospital. There was red tape in certain situations. Someone being at the house during the day, every day was annoying and felt so invasive. I know they didn't mean it that way, nevertheless this was something I wasn't used to. After each visit to the hospital, he would be discharged a couple of weeks later. Between all that happening, I had the other kids and their needs.

Ashley was gone most of the time from gymnastics, but when she came home, the reality of Michael's condition was a common reminder. Sam and Maddie had no idea about Michael and what was going on. They didn't understand. Remember, ignorance is bliss. At least, they wouldn't have any nightmares. I was exhausted from all of this with Michael, being a mother to the other kids and wife to someone who was unsupportive of me. I had the caregiver burn out, but when I tried to talk to him, he just walked away--he didn't get it.

By June 2013, Ashley went to camp solo this year and Michael would be at home. Ashley attended gymnastics 30 hours a week. There would be no MDA camp anymore. Michael condition was worsening each week, and I felt an ache in my heart that soon he may not be here. This is a heartache that no mother should have and will never get over. In late June, Manny's brother Adrian died from complications with diabetes. This was a sad moment that I thought would rattle Manny, but as usual--not one tear. He started to withdraw after this even more. I suggested therapy, like I had been saying all year, but he refused. This would be a decision he would regret later.

In August, the kids all went to school. Sam started kindergarten which was a milestone. She had some issues in preschool, but all the issues went away once she started school over here. In October, Maddie was diagnosed with a hearing loss which was caused by her condition at birth. She was placed in a prevention program with her preschool so she could learn sign language which she struggled with.

Maddie couldn't hear for all this time, so she would just nod. This was difficult to take in considering Michael was having such issues. Then to add to the stress, Sam had her tonsils out in early November. She did well with the surgery and was back at school in two weeks. Then things were calm once again, but only for a brief time. Things stayed interesting in our house.

The holidays came and went. We took a lot of pictures as always. The kids all looked so happy together. I looked around the house at all the pictures over the years of the children. Michael and Ashley have grown up so much. I look at Michael's pictures where he has no tubes and was just zooming around in his wheelchair. Then, I look now, and he has all this medical equipment. There were all these wires and tubes. Where does the time go? With my mind running through memory lane, I look at them opening their gifts and they all look so happy running around the house. They were all excited. The girls are always so eager to help Michael. I hope they will always be like that. I was blessed.

# CHAPTER TWENTY-SEVEN

## Losing The Fight

In January 2014, the kids all went back to school. Michael appeared to be weaker. In the next couple of weeks, the school called telling me how weak they noticed Michael was getting. Michael even started talking about how Megan and the family hadn't seen him and started asking if everything was, okay? I assured him that they were just busy with college and working. The week of January 19, 2014, Michael started saying how he would miss me and his sisters. I just smiled. Michael was losing his passion for life and the fight. He just didn't have it anymore. He was so weak, and he couldn't fight anymore. Michael started talking about Magic--the mysterious man from the cloud, that I say is an angel. Michael says he's been seeing him a lot. I knew at this moment that Michael was losing the will to live.

    I always said that we would fight, until Michael made the decision not to do so and we were at that point. All this fighting, you start to question what was the point? As a parent, it's hard to let go. With all the treatments, surgeries, therapies--there was nothing to stop this disease. It was relentless. When there is no cure, there is nothing a parent can do when your child is terminally ill. I prepare for the worst while I hope for the best and pray for a cure. It is torture to sit and watch him get weaker, but all you can do as a parent is to love your child and give him the best quality of life.

    Michael went to school on January 21, 2014, but missed the next two days because it was so cold. The air was bitter and so cold on January 24, 2014, when Michael went to sleep. I came in to check on him and he said Magic was here with him. I smiled and told him how much I loved him. There was a strong presence that we were not alone. I felt this warmness all over my body. Michael then started telling me he really wanted to go to college. He was a genius and should have gone to Harvard. Michael reminded me of Stephen Hawking, who went through so much with his condition, but overcame so much. Michael, however, would never get that chance. He fell asleep a while later. I went to put his clothes away at around 10pm. After I put them in the drawer, I went to check on Michael as I did every night, but this night felt different. He had his monitors vent going; they would beep every so often when his breathing patterns would change. We were all so used to hearing all the peeps and alarms that it was part of our life. Not hearing them would have been a different story.

I always wondered how it would happen. When would it happen? You are never prepared even if you know it's going to happen. Nothing can prepare you for the death of a child. The night was so cold and would become even colder. As I passed Michael's bed, I touched his forehead--it was ice cold. He was blue around the mouth and unresponsive. In a panic I called 911 and as I was on the phone Ashley came to the door. I had put Michael on the floor and began CPR, but I knew he was gone. A mother knows--my heart had dropped. I told her to go to her room, but she knew something was wrong. She screamed, "Michael, no Mommy." It looked like a CSI scene in front of the house, especially when it's a child. A few officers came running towards the door with two firefighters. I knew all of them. When they saw me at the door, one firefighter said, "It's Michael?" I shook my head, yes. They all went in and tried to help him. An officer I knew well asked all the questions they usually ask. An hour later, one of them came out and delivered the sad news. Michael died on January 24, 2014, at 10:28pm.

## CHAPTER TWENTY-EIGHT

# Gone Too Soon

As the words were being said, I just shut down. My baby Michael was gone. I wondered what his last moments were like, did you reach out for help? Did he see a light? Did his young life flash before his eyes? As I was being asked about a funeral home for Michael to be taken to, I had so many thoughts going through my head. I had the flashbacks of Michael rushing through my mind. I looked up at the wall and his pictures were all over the place from his birth, until just resent. With all the fighting we have done to keep him alive and all the treatment he has received, you wonder what it was for? You question things differently. Things have a unique perspective now. I feel like a bulldozer has just hit me a million times. For all the moments in the world that have been stollen, was the end results all worth it. No monument was built in his honor, no street was named after him, but our world will never be the same. My heart has shattered into a billion pieces. Michael was gone.

All I kept hearing in my head play repeatedly was "Michael was gone." My heart was broken in ways I cannot describe. I was so distant, a million miles from here. I was flying away from this place just like an eagle. Feeling so much pain that Michael was gone, and I couldn't see past his loss. My entire body was experiencing an ache— like I was being attacked. This was too overwhelming. I was crying--Ashley was crying. No matter how much you think because your child is terminally ill—that the blow comes softer. You better think again because it doesn't. Nothing in this world could have prepared me for this moment. My world will never be the same.

I was in such pain as a mother. Then I had to comfort my daughter who was in pain from the loss of her brother. This was a very intense emotional moment. I needed comfort from my husband, but he was not the comforting type. I needed that comfort more than ever to give me strength, so I can help the children with their grief. Ashley was old enough to understand, but Sam and Maddie would be questionable how much?

When Manny arrived, there were paramedics downstairs and he looked in the back of the ambulance, but Michael wasn't there. So, as he made it upstairs, he saw the police in the hallway. Manny walked into the living room and saw us crying. He went to the bedroom but was stopped. So, he walked by the window and slowly turned around. Just then the coroner walked in, and as Manny looked at him, he then looked slowly at me. He then started to question when Michael was going to be taken to the hospital, totally disregarding the grim reaper.

I was asked if I wanted to see him before he was taken to the funeral home. I went into his room that seemed colder than usual. There was a bright light shining in the room, with a shadow on the wall. It was a calming feeling. Then I knew the angels were all around. That's why Michael was seeing this man--he was an angel. I stayed silent with Michael, just thinking of all his years. I thought about the first moment I held him. Then the first steps he took and as he grew up, until now. As I looked down at his shoes, I remembered when he would walk around the house with my big shoes. My pain felt even deeper. I couldn't say goodbye to my Michael.

As a parent in pain, I of course wanted to play the conspiracy theory. I was unable to accept his heart just stopped or his lungs gave out. I wanted to blame something or someone for this tragedy. I know it won't bring him back, but I needed this moment to connect and vent. I went through everything that possibly could have happened. How could he just die? After all this, he was just gone. Michael's body was taken at 12:48am to Algrim's Funeral Home. It was late, so I didn't call anyone to tell anyone Michael was gone.

I stayed up the entire night. In the morning, I called Gale and let her know Michael passed away. Then the nurse Dawn showed up and she wasn't told anything by the nursing home care. When I told her, she just walked away. Then Manny called his mother and let her know. I forgot all about Ashley's gymnastics meet this morning, so her coach Mr. Hagel called, and he let me know the bus was waiting for her. I informed him that Ashley would not be coming because Michael was gone. I received over fifty calls within the hour from the school, as news spread that Michael had passed-away. They were asking about the arrangements. I just wanted to cry every time they asked that. Arrange what? My son was gone.

I went to the funeral home to make the so-called arrangements. I started to zone out when they wanted me to pick a casket, headstone, and location to be buried. Then there was the announcement, the prayer card, and the death certificate. The prayer card was difficult enough, but I chose, "I'm Free." which fitted Michael so well. He was finally free, to be the angel he was left to be. I had to believe this, just so I could have that moment of peace. But I lost it when they asked where I wanted Michael to be buried. I picked it in the kids' section, under a tree. There he would be free.

I went to go buy Michael a tie and a nice outfit to be laid to rest. When I came home Manny was with his family. I took him into the room to tell him the arrangements. Manny then started asking questions about last night. He then said, "Well, if I was here then this wouldn't have happened." That's him trying to play hero, as he disconnects himself from the emotion of the world. This was my son and he wanted to play interrogations with me. Manny started questioning if the alarm went off or if something was wrong. I shook my head and walked away. Michael was gone, but he wants to do this now. So, what was he saying, "It was my fault?" Where is compassion and comfort? I thought for one moment like this, that he could connect and act like a human being that loves me. But nope, he wants to blame. I was going through the emotions, and I was so angry that Michael was gone. My sadness was overwhelming, and my grief was growing. How could he just die on me like that?

On Wednesday, January 29, 2014, was Michael's wake. The wake was 2pm-6pm. Michael was laid to rest on January 30, 2014, at St. Michael's Cemetery. It was located across from Harper College. As

I walked in the funeral home, the funeral director Alan, said that they were going to open both rooms since there could be a lot of visitors. There were a lot of kids from the school, teachers, firefighters, police, and other community visitors. Then the MDA showed up to pay their respects to Michael.

Ashley's gymnastics team showed up but didn't say anything to her. I am sure this was a hard moment, and few knew what to say. Gale and her husband showed up with their younger son. They both gave me a hug and shared some words. Manny found a way to just distance himself, even at a time like this. There were no hugs and no comfort. This was a sad moment, and I wanted this day to be over. After everyone left and nobody was there, I walked up to the casket to look at my Michael. I looked down at him, he was peaceful and there were no wires or tubes. He was just my cute handsome Michael. I thought at any moment, he was going to jump up and say, "Just joking." As if this was some big prank, but that never happened. Maybe he was finally at peace. I still couldn't say goodbye.

The funeral was hard. Buses came from the schools around the area to say goodbye. This was so emotional, and I just wanted this day to go by fast. Michael's favorite song by Bon Jovi, "Living on a Prayer." The song suited him so well—he really was living on a prayer. The eulogy was read my Megan and to her dismay she did an exceptionally excellent job. She would always remember the day of his passing because it was her birthday. Michael felt abandoned at the end, mainly because they knew his fate. His end was near a year ago, just like Gale said at the hospital. I remember the doctor who warned me not to get the trach and other life-saving surgeries. He told me to let him go on his own. I wish I had that courage a year ago before this day. But it is what it is. The pallbearers consisted of Gale's younger son, and a few teachers from the school, including Mr. Hagel who was so warm to Ashley.

We drove to the cemetery on a freezing day to lay Michael to rest. We went into this little room and some prayers were said. Then because it was winter, Michael would be taken out to be buried without the funeral outside. Everyone said goodbye, but I just couldn't leave him. So, we drove around and found the spot where he was going to be buried. There were so many flowers for him. After waiting two hours, he was finally laid to rest. The flowers were placed on top.

This was an awful moment, and I can't believe this is happening. I felt totally ripped apart and isolated, as I had to manage my grief on my own. I still could bring myself to say goodbye.

Manny's family came to the house and Steve, who was Michael's old counselor, came along with him. His family ordered food, but I just walked away to my room. I had such grief running through me. They were laughing in the other room, and I wanted to believe that all people manage grief in a unique way. I was left with my thoughts. Ashley came into the room to hang out with me, but nothing could make us feel better. A thought I hadn't felt in a long time came to me, I just wanted to fly away.

That night I was just in bed when I heard Michael's alarms. So, not even thinking, I ran to the room, opened the door, and then realized he wasn't there. I turned on a light and just looked around at all this medical stuff. It was a clear reminder he was here along with all his memories. I felt a touch on my shoulder, so I turned. There was nobody there. As a mother who couldn't let go, I wanted to believe that Michael was here in the room. I felt his presence and scent all over the place. I asked God, to send me an angel. It was so hard when I would hear those alarms go off and Michael calling my name, "Mommy."

## CHAPTER TWENTY-NINE

# The Aftermath

The next week, I went into full mommy mode and took Sam and Ashley to grief counseling. Sam refused to go in the room since not understanding that Michael was gone. I allowed her to be the five-year-old she was. I knew in time she and Maddie would ask questions. Steve remained in contact with the family--checking in with us every month. Ashley struggled the most with the loss of Michael. She attended counseling at the school. We will call her counselor Eron. He really should be called Mr. I don't get it because he never did.

Looking at Mike's room--I didn't know what to do with everything. Was I going to be one of the parents who would leave the room untouched, or would I be one of the parents who wanted to pack up everything and redecorate? I was really struggling with looking into his room. It just haunted me. So, I packed his stuff up. I called the MDA to donate all his equipment and supplies. The supplies I had to throw away because they could not be donated, as they were no longer sterile. The equipment was donated, but it was a hard call make. After everything was picked up, me and Ashley painted the room green. But I missed Michael so much and I felt so much pain. How could life ever be the same? How could God let this happen? I don't understand why.

As time went by, we all grieved in diverse ways. Sam and Maddie didn't know a thing was out of place for the most part. Michael's absence was not a concern, mostly because he had absent moments like this before. Ashley remained in counseling and went through the phases of grief. I went through the phases. There was anger, sadness, acceptance, and moving forward. I was in the anger and sad phase. Sam was told Michael had died, but she just said, "Ok." I checked in with her every day, but she would just tell me about her day. Maddie was different though. She only had about a small percentage of hearing, currently. She had suffered a seizure a month ago and the cause was unknown. Maddie always acted like someone was there with her in the room.

Someone was talking to her. At first, I thought it was an imaginary friend, like a lot of kids have at this age. When Maddie was two years old, I would hear her talking to herself. I asked her to whom she was talking. She would always smile, and then show me some pictures she drew. They were always kids, except for one person. There was a man, with long black hair, who was dressed in white. He was always with her. She would have dream of this man, in the cloud, and she was a baby. She says, "He brought me to you, Mommy." But recently, she has been talking to someone.

She asked about Michael who she called, "Mic." When I asked, who she was talking to just days after Michael passed--she said Mic. She says, "Michael comes in her room every night and sits on her bed. He wasn't in a wheelchair anymore. He would take her by the hand and lead her to the door. After that I wake up." She knows, the man. As she refers to the man in the cloud. Michael knew a man in the cloud as well. What is it with the man in the cloud? The strange thing is, I have found Maddie by the door a few times now. Other days, she would make up with night terrors, screaming. Perhaps, Michael is here.

But the other day, she said the kids wanted to play with her. She said this in front of Ashley, who just looked. A little offended that Michael would come to see her only. So, a few weeks after Michael passed, she called me into the room. She pointed and said, "Do you see them." I looked around and didn't see anything. Then she looked back at me, pulled out a picture, and pointed to it. Maddie didn't care to explain it. But, then after that she went into a closet and was digging through some items, we kept that belonged to Michael; he pulled out a bear that Michael used to carry around, called, "Bouncy

Bouncy Bear." She was in her room playing with it when I walked in. Maddie was carrying on playing while talking to someone. When I asked her, to whom she was talking? She said, "Mike wanted his bear. Oh, he wanted to know where the cowboy hat was. Do you know Mommy?" My only assumption was that Michael was there with her and she was talking to him. This bear was old, and she would have never known about the hat because his hat disappeared before she was born. Oh my--Michael is here.

Over the next few months, she would tell me that Mike was with her and the man. She also would talk about other kids. After a while, Ashley would say Maddie has some new friends. She wanted to have a playdate. Ashley would quickly smile and say, "Are these friends alive?" I would quickly say, "Ashley I don't know." The truth is Maddie may not understand what she is seeing. Are they alive or dead? Did Maddie have a highly creative imagination? Was this her way of dealing with the grief? There are no easy answers. Did Maddie have the light? It seems she was always talking to someone, so I decided to make an appointment with the doctor.

There were triggers that we had to avoid. There was no going by the cemetery and funeral home. These two places carried a different meaning now. It brought great sadness, and I would just burst into tears if I came across these places. Also, movies and television, I had to avoid anything with death. I couldn't handle this at all. Ashley had the same triggers. I didn't talk about Michael's passing with anyone. But people who lived in my condominium building tried to say the most insensitive words to me. One lady said, "Well, finally you let him go. Keeping him alive was wrong." Another last said, "Well I had a miscarriage, so I totally understand." A little different than watching your son grow weaker and then pass-away. Sometimes, silence is golden. During this time, I just withdrew from everyone, except my kids. I blacked out on all social media. I wanted to protect myself from seeing anything that would trigger these painful feelings.

By May 2014, Ashley was told by her school that she had to move forward through the grieving process. Ashley had grieved for a few months, but now she needed to be done. So, she had a time limit on grieving for her brother? This was insane. The school set the rules for a child's grieving process. Ashley was struggling with her education, gymnastics, and the feeling of great sadness over the loss of her brother. She withdrew from most people at her school. Other kids and teachers would just look at her. They would stare and then whisper saying, "She's Michael's little sister." This all made her feel so uncomfortable. She would have crying spells at school. Ashley was lonely for friendship, but she had nobody at school she could connect with. She missed her brother so much. We didn't know how we would ever get through this.

On June 3, 2014, I took Ashley and Sam to the cemetery to pay respects to Mike. We also started a tradition-- to let up in the sky red balloons for the number of years he would have been. This was in honor of Michael. But we extended it to all sons that have been lost to DMD, and everything else. A loss is a loss and causes the same amount of pain. All children that have been taken from their parents leave them heartbroken. For a mother, I know the pain all too well. I see his life as it was from the moment, I held him in my arms to the moment he left them. This is how we can honor them with red balloons and great positive inspiring stories of their legacies.

The first year of a loss is always the hardest. The holidays create such grief for us. It was pure agony for me. A pain I don't wish upon anyone. I missed his smiles and the way he said mommy. It had such energy to it. He will always be my Michael. As life presses on, we were stuck in the moment of grief, while the world moved forward with life. Life goes on for everyone else, except for the ones experiencing grief. I felt at times that everyone just forgot about him and just moved on. It really is our loss. The outsiders and people who Michael touched their lives were sad for the moment, but then again, life goes on.

After the death, Megan and her family disappeared. Megan came to take Ashley shopping, and the three other kids never spoke to Ashley again. Gale continued to pay for Ashley's gymnastics for which she was gracious. My goddaughter never spoke to Ashley again. There was no support to Ashley after the death and there was no check-ins. She felt abandoned by people she thought would never do that. Everyone feels bad for the one who passed, a sweet little boy, named Michael. But it's the survivors who need the support.

Our pain goes on for a while. I felt abandoned too and that feeling got even worse when I got the call from my goddaughter, who called not to offer condolences, but to borrow money from me. Support is a two-way street, so when she walked away from being a caring, decent, and loving human-being--I closed that door forever. Once I close that door, I never reopen it.

I didn't even know what to do with myself. I never realized just how much time I spent with Michael--taking care of all his needs. But once he was gone--I felt so lost. There were other kids in the house. Then I started to see my marriage for what it really was. Emotionally, I separated from my partner, and I watched this for a while, but was scared to do anything about it. If I learned anything from Michael--life is too short. You must enjoy life, find happiness and peace. I had to learn to cut the toxic people out of my life who interrupted my peace.

Samantha realized two years after Michael's passing that he was really gone. She pulled us through the grieving process again. That was hard, but Ashley was a great big sister and was there to give those hugs. Maddie realized Michael was gone after all her treatment was done. Soon after that Maddie started to hear things. Six months later, she had almost 80% in both ears. The doctors couldn't explain it. But at least this was a positive thing for our family. However, Maddie was diagnosed with a learning disability that could improve over time and Asperger's syndrome, but functional. She has her moments, but she has come such a long way. Often the school would say how she was not at the same level as her peers. I didn't like it when they would do this to Maddie. What should be said, find a child who went through all that Maddie has gone through, then start comparing them. That usually shuts them up. I want to believe time will ease the pain, but time will never heal my heartache. There will be a part of me that will never be the same.

Michael taught me to always look forward, never complain about your differences even if they are difficult, and always be humble to the greatest gift of life. He taught me to love and to be loved unconditionally. In addition, he reminded me to be happy for each day that we live, not to give up and fight until that will to live, leaves your body. Once you have a child who suffered through the terminal illness of Muscular Dystrophy, it prepares you for anything. As Maddie was diagnosed with some, not so pretty in pink conditions, I knew the strength that was needed to get through. The family will be guided by the light and our inner strength. At the end of the day, all we have is our faith and our ambition to find peace. I know one day, I will find the acceptance of Michael's loss, I will be able to say goodbye, and be at peace. I will not feel the guilt for Michael's death and know that there are things I will never understand. Some aspects of life are out of my control, and I don't blame God for that. Perhaps, God had great plans for Michael, and it makes me feel better to think of Michael as an angel.

When I remember you, my son Michael, I remember the smile that lit up the room. I remember, the love you had for life, the eagerness to love everyone. I remember the love you spread to the world. I remember the way you smiled, and your eyes lit up the sky. I remember your will for life and the fight you had to the end. I remember your ambition for the world, your personality of conspiracy, and your hunger to learn about all humankind. Thank you, for blessing our lives. I know you're in heaven looking down.

## CHAPTER THIRTY

## NEVER CAN SAY GOODBYE

Loss is an exceedingly difficult thing for anyone to cope with and deal with the terrible grief that drowns your heart and soul. Losing a child feels like part of you has died. It's so hard to grieve when you have other children that need you. You just can't be sad all day, so you have to be strong. Sometimes, this means neglecting your feelings and to emerge yourself in helping your children grieve.

Life at the moment never seems like it will ever be the same as you might once have known it. Like I said before, my heart shattered into a billion pieces, and I don't even know where the pieces are to mend back. There really is no going back to the way things were before I lost my Michael. I found myself just emerging in him more, just to feel him and be close to him.

There were things I just couldn't do anymore, and I didn't think I would ever recover from my loss, and my grief that was overwhelming. My love for Michael didn't cease when he was no longer here with me. I couldn't pass by any funeral home, especially the one that he was at. I couldn't watch any movies that had death or funerals in them. There were no horror movies either. Death was something much deeper. Every waking moment I saw cars come drive in their parade going to a funeral, I wondered if it was a child. I prayed that it was not. No parent should watch their child grow weaker and then just be no more. The last moments haunted me like a bad nightmare that wouldn't go away. At this moment, me and God are not on the same page, once again. How could he take my Michael? I could not hear that he had a bigger plan for my son, at least not right now. I would take his Blue's Clues blanket wrap it around me, then I would watch Connan, Harry Potter movies, CSI, and all his other shows. Then I would listen to Living on a Prayer over and over. Sitting I would visualize happy moments from birth until things just went all wrong with this disease. Sometimes I would laugh and then it would turn to me crying. I felt at times, I was having a challenging time controlling my emotions. But all this was normal. The grieving process is hard, especially when it's your child. He was my baby. I miss him so much, and I am not ready to let him go. I can't say goodbye—I just can't. I don't think a mother really ever gets over losing her child. I know time heals—so they say. But for now, I will keep him close to me by any means I can. I have to keep those precious moments and the most loving ones close to my heart. These are the treasures that humble me. I know he is finally free of this world, his pain, and his disease. But he is so missed. I never can say goodbye, Michael.

My son Michael was gone. That's a deep wound that will never heal. He was my precious little angel and always there with a grand smile for me. But now he was no more. I had to neglect myself from going through the phases or perhaps just postpone it a bit. So, there was phase 1: the silent anger I had to hide and only write about in my journal. There was Phase 2: acceptance which I really struggled with. Why should I accept that my son was gone when I already know that. I found my son lifeless, had to call 911, and watch as my child was wheeled out of the house. Then I had to watch him be buried. I then watched Ashley fall apart day by day because she grieved so hard. The other children didn't understand as I have already pointed out. I accepted my son was gone, but then I had to revisit the anger part and the reasons I was angry at for real.

Then I had to deal with the people who wanted to bring God into this. This was not the moment. But I had to deal with when the unexplained needs an explanation and there is none—time to call for God. Let their child die and we will see how godly they feel. The pain I felt was overwhelming and I had no one to share it with. My husband lived in his own little world full of emotionless antisocial nonsense. This created a wedge a few years before that seemed to break us apart.

This started years before Michael passed away that night. So, there was no support. I had to blame someone and something for what had occurred. God let me down at that moment. The disease was so relentless, so at this time I hate Muscular Dystrophy, especially Duchenne's. I felt alone in my pain and was sick of people who had not lost a child or loved one to this or a similar terminal illness--giving them empty minded moments. Just let me grieve. I have the right to be angry and miss my son. And I deeply missed Michael so much.

I can say that life after Michael was so challenging. It was like part of my heart died. I didn't feel that life would ever be the same. But I also knew I had other children in the house, so I had to pull it together. That's the major issue when you are titled the strong one. People around think you can just deal with anything. I needed private moments to allow myself to grieve. I needed time. Eventually, I got through.

Michael, gone too soon.

# Michael

Michael, you are the sweetest child that can be.

You lit up everyone's world with that smile

My love, you were such a blessing in those short years.

My son, you showed the world how to live and love.

I know you suffered, but never complained.

Gone, but not forgotten.

Michael, I hope you are at peace.

Michael, you will always be remembered.

As I hear softly, your sweet voice.

I shall remember all the hugs and kisses.

Michael, you are like the birds that fly over the sea.

You are finally free.

# Author's Note

As I started to pull all my writings from all my journals to draft this book, I struggled with great emotion. I started and stopped many times before getting to the point that I could really get this project done. I had to think back to my many conversations with Michael. This caused me to pull from what he would have wanted. Just like when any child passes away from a terminal illness, we think of how to honor that person. But there are challenges to who you are, your beliefs, and how this has changed you. So, I drafted the book in three months and then could not bear to write the chapter where he passes way or the chapters therefore after. It would take me two years to come back and finish this book and write the children's memory book. I had to really push myself to complete these projects to share with the world our story about Michael.

# Epilogue

Michael had a rough journey filled with moments of love, understanding, frustration, and acceptance. I know what it is about Michael's? They light up the world with their smile, talent, or with their energy. At the end, I always like to reflect on what happened, the journey itself and what was learned from it. When it first happened, I often would think about Michael's last moments and they go something like this. Did he cry out or reach out? Did his life flash before his eyes? What was this moment like? I pray he did not have any pain. I used to think of this all the time, and as I grieved, I had to allow myself moments like this. Then as time passed, I had to allow myself to be angry, sad, accept, and work towards peace. I needed and deserved peace.

There's the journey of healing, and the climb towards peace. I came to the conclusion that death is hard. It is the people who are left behind that feel the pain of the loss of a loved one. I felt so imperfect having these emotions while trying to be controlled emotionally. This pain was enormous, and it just consumed me. Why me? Why my Michael? But no one on the outside or even the kids could see what I was going through. Being the strong one at this moment did nothing more than help others to not see you as human, but a superhero. Even strong people have moments of despair, anger, and my grief was eating me up alive. So, my outlet was writing my heart out. After losing a child my world was damaged emotionally and spiritually.

Part of me just died when Michael died. The lights just went dark. I was just merely here walking on Earth. My heart and soul were just burning. I felt when it happened, that how would I find my way back to living. My daughters were part of that life, so I had to force myself to focus on the positive and the future that would not include

Michael. As unfair as it was, I had to force myself to move forward. Life goes on. But in that, I had to give myself permission to be happy and to have fun. I was even upset that my little boy died. How could he just die on me like that? After all this, is it just over? Was it worth it? He fought so hard. We fought so hard, but in the end was there a point? Life is life. The lesson that is true will always remain that life is short. Live life to the fullest. So, maybe in Michael's short legacy—a street was not named after him nor was there a cure found or named after him. His mark in this world was the fact that even know he had this terrible disease, he lived, he loved, he smiled, and laughed back at a disease merely saying—you are not going to take my joy of living. That is a remarkable gift and message for everyone.

Life is what you make it to be. Live life until the end to the fullest. You just have to live. Death is complete, make sure you leave no unanswered questions. Make sure your journey is complete with only peace in your heart.

Stay Calm--Make a Muscle--Find a Cure--Fight Muscular Dystrophy.

For more information about Muscular Dystrophy.

Contact
Muscular Dystrophy Association
1016 W Jackson Blvd #1073
Chicago, IL 60607
1(800)-572-1717
RecourceCenter@mdausa.org

# Acknowledgements

The fact that this book exists feels utterly impossible and it would not have been possible without the incredible love and support of my family and friends.

Thank you to my daughters for always being so supportive. Thank you, to the MDA, for always giving support to our family.

Thank you to Quest Magazine for always keeping up updated on equipment and new treatments in the MDA world.

Thank you to Geri, David, and Mac for being supportive while Michael was here with us.

Thank you to all the non-profit organizations that give their time, love and support to families who are either battling the disease themselves or have a loved one who is being impacted.

Thank you to all the doctors, nurses and other medical professionals who treated Michael at his time of need and showed love, kindness, and dedication.

www.ingramcontent.com/pod-product-compliance
Lightning Source LLC
LaVergne TN
LVHW021824060526
838201LV00058B/3496